SEWING
FOR KIDS

SEWING FOR KIDS

**Alice Butcher and
Ginny Farquhar**

David and Charles

www.stitchcraftcreate.co.uk

contents

Hello and Welcome to...

SEWING FOR KIDS

Let us introduce ourselves: our names are Alice and Ginny and we are sewing teachers. We love making things with fabric and have both been sewing since we were very young.

We really enjoy encouraging young people, just like you, to learn how to sew and have designed this book filled with fun projects for you to make, including scary softies, fruity juggling balls, rainbow bunting, felt dress up dolls, your first patchwork quilt and lots more! If you are new to sewing, you will need to work with an adult but once you have learnt some of the basic skills and stitches, you will soon become more independent.

Throughout the book you will find a cotton reel companion called Sylky who will give you lots of useful tips and advice. Each project contains a 'You will learn' box, telling you the main skill being taught and a 'What you will need' list, advising you of all the materials you will require. It's a good idea to read through the instructions and look at the pictures with an adult before you begin. We have provided step-by-step drawings and don't forget to look at the finished picture of the project to help you.

Learning to sew is an enjoyable adventure and collecting materials to use is an exciting part of it. Start a fabric scrap box by saving material from old clothes – recycling is good for the environment and can save you money. Collect embellishments such as ribbons, buttons and sequins, which can add a lovely finishing touch to your projects.

Most of our projects have been made from cotton or felt and all have been designed to be sewn by hand. Some could also be sewn using a sewing machine (see Sewing Machine Basics for tips).

We hope you have lots of fun making the projects!

Alice and Ginny x

Make sure your hands are clean and work on a clear, flat surface.

Pack ongoing projects away in a bag to prevent them getting lost or dirty.

It's okay to make mistakes because that is how you learn. Simply undo the mistake and start again.

top tips

You do not have to make the project in the same colours as shown. It's fun to get creative and use your own favourite colours.

Make the projects your own – you may not wish to make an entire project, such as the Boys Versus Girls game, but may just prefer to just make up some of the faces.

It's good to ask for help from an adult or older sibling. You may need help initially with threading needles and tying knots but once practised, you can do this unaided.

Take your time and don't rush – you don't have to finish the project in one go. Some projects will be quick but others may take a number of weeks to complete.

Your stitches don't have to be perfect – you will improve with practice.

Take great care when using scissors, pins and needles, as they are very sharp!

HanDy sewing Kit

THIS BASIC KIT CONTAINS MANY OF THE ESSENTIAL HABERDASHERY
ITEMS THAT YOU WILL NEED FOR THE PROJECTS IN THIS BOOK.

Scissors

Dressmaking scissors (shears)

It is important to have a pair of sharp dressmaking scissors.
Make sure you only use them for sewing as they will get
blunt; use general-purpose scissors for cutting paper.

Embroidery scissors

A smaller pair of embroidery scissors can be used
for trimming fabric and cutting threads.

Pinking shears

Pinking shears have a serrated edge and
are used to trim seam
edges and prevent
fabric from fraying.

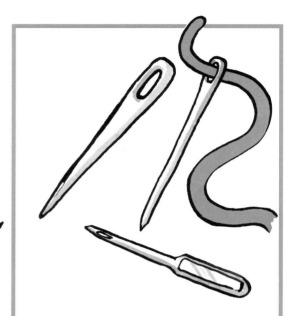

Threads

Multi-purpose polyester thread

Suitable for hand and machine sewing, this comes
in a huge variety of colours. It can be used with all
fabrics and has more stretch than cotton threads so
won't snap as easily.

Topstitching thread

Thicker than normal thread, this can be used when
you need a stronger thread. It is recommended for
most of the hand-sewn projects in this book.

Embroidery skeins

Embroidery skeins or threads come in lots
of different colours and can be used for
both embroidery and hand stitching.
Made from six threads twisted
together, they can be split to two or
three threads for easier sewing.

Hand sewing needles

Tapestry needles

Tapestry needles are quite thick with
a large eye and a sharp point, ideal
for using with embroidery silks or
thick sewing threads.

Embroidery needles

These come in a variety of sizes. They
are slimmer than tapestry needles,
allowing for use on finer fabrics but
they still have a large eye, making
them easy to thread.

Sharps

These are versatile, medium-length,
general sewing needles, built with a
sharp point and a round eye.

Sewing machine needles

Different sizes are suitable for
different fabrics, from size 70 for
fine fabrics through to size 100 for
heavyweight fabrics. Change them
regularly as they can get blunt.

Fabric Markers

Dressmaker's pencils
These mark out fabric clearly and because they are made with chalk, the markings will easily brush away.

Vanishing markers
This can be used like a felt tip to mark or draw outlines on fabric. Because they are light sensitive, they will fade and disappear after a few days.

Water erasable pen
This can be used like the vanishing marker however the markings are removed with water.

Sewing accessories

Plastic headed pins
These are simple to put in and pull out of fabric and are easily visible for sewing and picking up off the floor!

Tape measure
It is useful to have one that displays both centimetres and inches and is made from vinyl so it won't stretch.

Thimble
A thimble is really useful when hand sewing as it protects your fingers from getting pricked by the needle. They come in different sizes and should be worn on either the index or middle finger.

Pincushion and needle case
These are useful to keep your pins and needles safe. Why not make your own pincushion (see Sylky the Sewing Mate)?

Bondaweb (double-sided fusible webbing)
This is a double-sided iron-on fabric adhesive that comes on peel-off paper backing, perfect for crafting and appliqué.

Toy stuffing
This is essential for stuffing your softies and other toys, such as the Pentagon Patchwork Ball.

Other useful items
It is also handy to have a soft pencil, ruler, rubber, tracing paper, paper and card for making patterns and templates.

"A sewing box is useful for storing your kit. You can buy pretty sewing boxes but a wrapped shoebox or biscuit tin would do just as well!"

things to know Before you start

THE FOLLOWING HINTS AND TIPS WILL INTRODUCE YOU TO THE BASICS AND GIVE YOU THE ESSENTIAL SEWING KNOW-HOW THAT YOU WILL NEED TO TACKLE THE PROJECTS IN THIS BOOK AND BEYOND.

Templates

All of the templates are full size and can be found within the project pages. To copy them, use a photocopier or place tracing paper (or thin paper) over them and trace around the outline with a pencil. Each template is labelled and advises how many to cut out, e.g. x 2. To cut out two of the same template, fold your piece of fabric in half, pin on the template and cut out carefully.

Patterns

If a project requires a pattern, measurements are given. Draw them onto paper using a pencil and ruler.

Markings

You will find dashes and dots on some of the templates. Use a chalk pencil or fabric marker to transfer them. Lift the edge of the template away from the fabric and mark onto the wrong side.

Threading a needle

Needles have a hole at one end called an eye. To thread the needle, neatly cut off a length of sewing thread, about 50cm (20in) long. Hold up your needle vertically with the eye facing you. Hold your thread about 1cm (⅜in) from the end and carefully guide it through the eye, pulling through to the other side. To help you, cut the end of your thread at a 45-degree angle or wet the end. For most projects you will use a single thread but for sewing on buttons make a double thread by pulling the two ends together and tying a knot.

Fabric

Most of the projects have been made from either cotton or felt. Cotton is a natural fabric that is easy to work with as it doesn't stretch or slip. Felt does not fray and comes in lots of different colours.

The right side of your fabric (R/S) is the side you want to be on the outside of your project. On a printed fabric this is easy to recognize but on a plain fabric you may have to decide which side this is. The wrong side (W/S) is the side you want to be on the inside of your project.

How to cut out fabric
Always press (iron) the fabric first to remove creases, using a pressing cloth over felt to prevent scorching.

Pin your pattern/template onto the fabric, using enough pins to keep everything flat. Using dressmaking scissors, cut out your fabric with long strokes on a flat surface, keeping the scissors close to the table or draw around the template, remove pins then cut out.

Starting and finishing off stitches

Starting off stitches
Either tie a knot at the end of your thread or sew a few small stitches on the wrong side of the fabric at the starting point.

Finishing off stitches
Bring the needle to the wrong side of the fabric and secure the thread with two small stitches. On the last stitch, as you pull the thread through, push the needle through the loop to create a knot. Cut off the threads.

Hand sewing

All of the projects are designed to be hand sewn and the instructions will tell you which stitches to use and where to stitch (the stitching line). When two pieces of fabric are sewn together it creates a seam. The distance from the stitch line to the edge of the fabric is called the seam allowance and specific seam allowances will be given in each project. Don't forget to pin before you sew to keep everything in place.

The three main stitches used are running stitch, backstitch and overstitch (see Stitch Library):

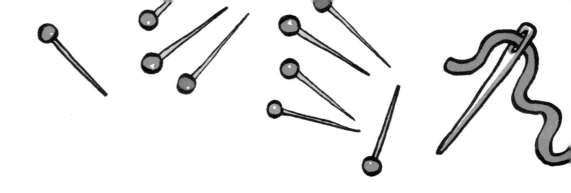

• **Running stitch** is a short, even stitch that can be used for sewing two pieces of fabric together, gathering fabric or adding decoration.

• **Backstitch** is a stronger stitch, ideal for sewing two pieces of fabric together when sewing seams or as an outline embroidery stitch.

• **Overstitch** is used to sew up gaps and can sew seams together from the right side.

Pressing (ironing)

Using an iron is an important part of sewing, however we advise that you never use an iron unsupervised. Extreme caution must be taken as irons are very hot and you should always ask an adult's permission first.

Pressing is important for removing creases, straightening open seams and turning under edges to give a nice finish. Always check the fabric instructions before setting the temperature – if the iron is too hot it could burn your fabric. A pressing cloth is essential. It needn't be expensive; just a large square of muslin will help protect your fabric and your iron.

Sewing on a button

1 Secure the thread onto the back of the fabric with a few small stitches and push the needle through to the front.

2 Thread the needle up through one hole of the button and then push it back down to the back of the fabric through the diagonal hole. Sew through the holes three times then cross over to the remaining holes and repeat, making sure that you don't pull the thread too tight.

3 Finish on the back with a couple of small stitches. On the last stitch, push the needle through the loop and pull tight to create a knot. Cut off the remaining thread.

Using Bondaweb

1 Lay the Bondaweb (double-sided fusible webbing) over your drawn template/design with the paper (smooth) side up. Trace the design using a pencil.

2 Cut out the shape roughly, leaving a 5mm (¼in) border – do not cut on the pencil line! Place the Bondaweb glue (rough) side down onto the back of the fabric, cover with a pressing cloth and with an adult's help, set the iron to hot and press for five seconds.

3 Carefully cut out on the pencil line. Peel off the paper backing and position your design glue side down onto the item you wish to decorate. Cover with the pressing cloth and press into place.

sewing Machine Basics

A SEWING MACHINE IS AN ELECTRICALLY POWERED MACHINE DESIGNED TO SEW STITCHES, PRODUCING QUICKER, NEATER AND STRONGER RESULTS. IT USES TWO THREADS: ONE AT THE TOP OF THE MACHINE CALLED THE SPOOL, WHICH IS THREADED THROUGH THE NEEDLE AND ONE UNDERNEATH CALLED THE BOBBIN, WHICH SITS IN THE BOBBIN CASE. THE STITCHES ARE CREATED WHEN THE TWO THREADS INTERLINK.

Sewing machine know-how

✓ Always ask an adult's permission before using a sewing machine. Don't use one on your own until an adult says you are safe to do so.

✓ If you are unsure of anything, always ask for help.

✓ Sewing machines are electrically powered. Always switch the machine off when you are threading it or changing a needle.

✓ If the machine makes a funny noise or jams, turn off the power and seek assistance.

✓ Sit in an upright, comfortable position with the machine directly in front of you and the foot pedal within easy reach.

✓ Sew slowly and with care, keeping your fingers away from the moving needle. If your machine has a slow setting, set it to this.

✓ Never sew over pins.

✓ Do not have food and drink near your sewing area.

✓ Tie long hair back.

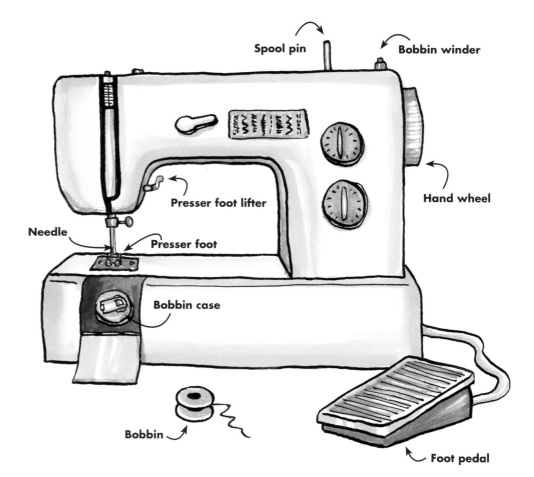

Spool pin

Bobbin winder

Presser foot lifter

Hand wheel

Needle

Presser foot

Bobbin case

Bobbin

Foot pedal

"Practise on scrap fabric first. Always refer to the instruction manual or ask an adult for help."

Setting up your machine

1 To wind the bobbin, push the thread though the hole at the top. Put the bobbin onto the winder and press the foot pedal until the bobbin is full. Cut off the threads and put it in the bobbin case.

2 Most sewing machines thread up in a similar way but refer to your manual for clear instructions. Thread the needle from front to back.

3 Pick up the bobbin thread by moving the hand wheel towards you in one full rotation. The needle goes down into the machine and the top thread loops around the bobbin to pull up the bottom thread. If you pull gently on the top thread, the loop of the bottom thread appears and can be pulled through.

Beginning to sew

1 Sew with a straight stitch. If you have a stitch length control, set it to 2.5. Make sure the two threads are long and place them under the presser foot.

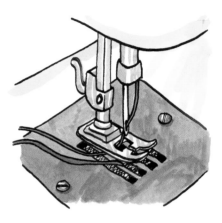

2 With the bulk of the fabric to the left, lower the presser foot to hold it in place.

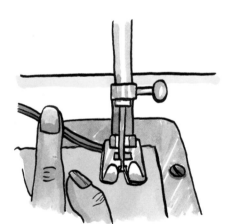

3 To sew in a straight line, use the edge of the presser foot as a guide. Alternatively, measure the required seam allowance to the right of the needle, stick on a piece of masking tape and follow the edge.

4 Turn the hand wheel towards you to lower the needle into the fabric. It should *always* turn towards you to avoid jamming the machine. Guide the fabric lightly with your hands and do not pull. Keep your hands well away from the moving needle. Gently press the foot pedal to start stitching.

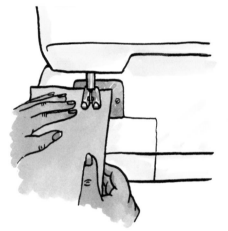

5 At the beginning and end of a stitching line, press in your reverse lever to secure the stitches.

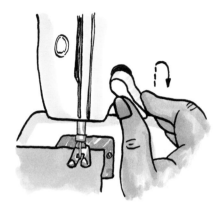

6 To turn a corner, check the needle is in the down position, lift the presser foot, turn the fabric, lower the presser foot and continue. To sew along a curve, you may need to lift the presser foot and slightly move the fabric.

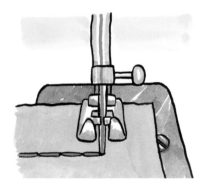

7 To remove your fabric from the machine, finish with the needle in the up position, lift the presser foot and pull the fabric out towards the back. Cut off the threads.

sylky the sewing mate

INSPIRED BY SYLKY, YOUR HELPFUL COMPANION THROUGHOUT THE BOOK, THIS SOFTIE COTTON REEL SERVES A DOUBLE PURPOSE AS A PINCUSHION AND A NEEDLE CASE. IT IS READY TO ASSIST YOU WITH ALL YOUR SEWING ADVENTURES!

"Collect buttons from your old clothing to build up a button box."

✎ **What you will need** • FELT IN STONE 20 × 40CM (8 × 16IN), WHITE 10 × 20CM (4 × 8IN), OLIVE GREEN 10CM (4IN) SQUARE, PINK 10CM (4IN) SQUARE, AND A SCRAP OF BROWN • ONE 1.5CM (⅝IN) BROWN BUTTON • ONE POPPER AND SNAP • EMBROIDERY THREAD IN NAVY, BROWN AND STONE • OLIVE GREEN YARN, 5.75M (19FT) LENGTH

1 Pin and cut out templates A–E in the felt colours indicated. Sew one label (C) onto one reel piece (B) with running stitch in navy thread. Sew on a button (see stitch panel) at the centre. Sew through the holes three times then cross over to the remaining holes and repeat. Finish on the back with small stitches. Push the needle through the loop on the last stitch, pull to knot and cut off thread.

2 On the second label (C), sew the hole piece (D) onto the centre with an overstitch. Position onto the second reel piece (B) and running stitch together using navy thread.

Sewing on a button

3 Fold the sides of reel (A) in half so the short sides meet. Pin and running stitch a 1cm (⅜in) seam along the short sides in stone thread. Turn through to the front.

4 Take the last reel piece (B) and pin onto one end of the side of the reel then running stitch together. Take the pink and green pages (E) for the needles and the decorated reel piece (B) with button. Pin and running stitch through all layers to attach to the back of the reel.

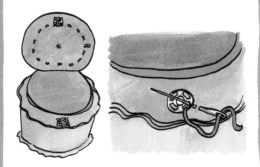

5 Sew the completed felt circle with hole piece (D) to the other end, leaving a gap for stuffing. Stuff loosely and sew up the gap. On the front edge of the reel, sew a popper to the base and flap, attaching with overstitches.

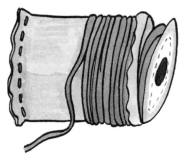

6 Take the yarn, sew in place with a few overstitches then wind evenly around the reel. Sew in place with a few stitches then cut, leaving a 4cm (1¾in) thread.

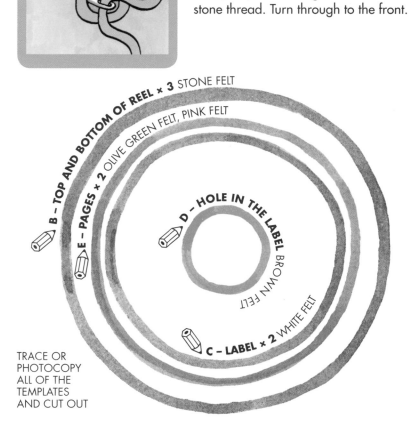

B – TOP AND BOTTOM OF REEL × 3 STONE FELT

E – PAGES × 2 OLIVE GREEN FELT, PINK FELT

D – HOLE IN THE LABEL BROWN FELT

C – LABEL × 2 WHITE FELT

A – SIDE OF REEL STONE FELT

TRACE OR PHOTOCOPY ALL OF THE TEMPLATES AND CUT OUT

Rainbow Bunting

THIS STRING OF COLOURFUL RAINBOW BUNTING WILL BRIGHTEN UP EVEN THE CLOUDIEST OF DAYS! THE PLAIN FLAGS GIVE YOU A CHANCE TO GET CREATIVE BY ADDING YOUR OWN DELIGHTFUL DRAWINGS AND DESIGNS.

✏️ **What you will need** • COTTON FABRIC IN RED, YELLOW, ORANGE, GREEN, LIGHT BLUE, INDIGO AND VIOLET, EACH PIECE 34 × 20CM (13½ × 8IN) • PLAIN NATURAL-COLOURED COTTON FABRIC 1 × 0.2M (40 × 8IN) • 2CM (¾IN) WIDTH COTTON TAPE, 2M (80IN) • IVORY TOPSTITCHING THREAD (FOR HAND SEWING) OR POLYESTER MULTIPURPOSE THREAD (FOR MACHINE SEWING) • VANISHING FABRIC PEN • FABRIC PENS OR CRAYONS • PENCIL

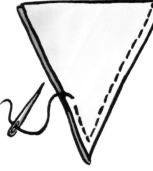

1 Fold a piece of coloured fabric in half, pin on template A and cut out. Repeat to cut six more pairs of different coloured flags and six pairs of plain flags.

2 Place the first pair of flags right (front) sides together. Place template B centrally inside the flag and draw on the stitching line.

3 Pin the flags together and sew by hand with a backstitch (see stitch panel) or using a sewing machine.

5 Repeat steps 2 and 3 with all of your flags. Then use coloured fabric pens to decorate the plain flags with simple drawings of rainclouds, the sun and rainbows.

6 Fold the cotton tape in half, insert the flags and attach with running stitch. Hang up and enjoy!

4 Trim the seam allowance at the tip of the flag to create a point. Turn the flag through to the right side and ask an adult to help you press (iron) it.

B – STITCHING GUIDE

A – FLAG

TRACE OR PHOTOCOPY THE TEMPLATES AND CUT OUT

"Old striped cotton shirts would look great as bunting."

spooky softies

"Why not have a go at drawing up your own designs for other characters?"

THESE SPOOKY SOFTIES ARE GREAT FOR HALLOWEEN FUN! FOR THE SCARY MONSTER, THREE BODY SECTIONS ARE ATTACHED BEFORE IT IS ALL SEWN TOGETHER WITH RUNNING STITCH. THE SPOOKY GHOST IS PERFECT FOR BEGINNERS – QUICK AND EASY TO STITCH IN ONE PIECE.

✏️ **What you will need** • **FOR THE GHOST:** FELT IN WHITE 50 × 30CM (20 × 12IN) AND A SCRAP OF BLACK • BLACK EMBROIDERY THREAD • TOY STUFFING **FOR THE MONSTER:** FELT IN GREY 15 × 30CM (6 × 12IN), DARK BROWN 20 × 30CM (8 × 12IN), GREEN 30 × 40CM (12 × 16IN), SCRAPS OF LIGHT BROWN AND WHITE • TWO BLACK OR GREY BUTTONS • BLACK EMBROIDERY THREAD • VANISHING FABRIC PEN

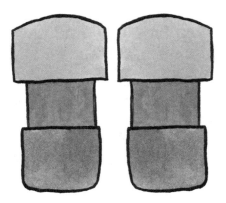

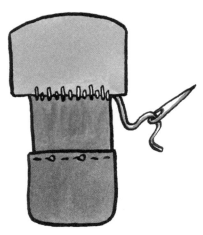

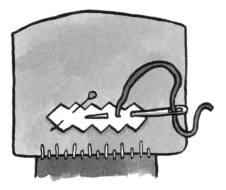

1 For the monster softie, pin and cut out templates A–F in the felt colours indicated. Lay body pieces A, B and C out in a mirror image.

2 Overlap each section by 1cm (⅜in), pin and sew using a long straight stitch (see Stitch Library).

3 Sew on the mouth using backstitch and the patch using straight overstitch.

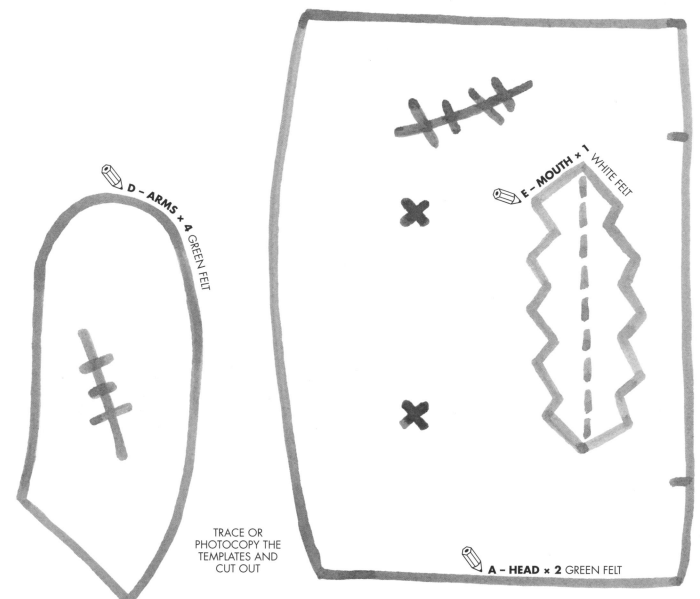

🖊 **D – ARMS × 4** GREEN FELT

TRACE OR PHOTOCOPY THE TEMPLATES AND CUT OUT

🖊 **E – MOUTH × 1** WHITE FELT

🖊 **A – HEAD × 2** GREEN FELT

✏ **B – BODY × 2** GREY FELT

4 On one arm, draw the stitch detail in vanishing fabric pen. Backstitch along the line and repeat for the stitches on the head. Pin both pairs of arms together and running stitch around (see stitch panel). Stuff well, leaving the top 1cm (⅜in) clear (unstuffed).

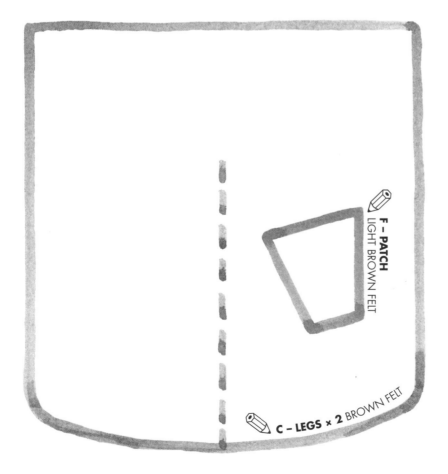

✏ **F – PATCH** LIGHT BROWN FELT

✏ **C – LEGS × 2** BROWN FELT

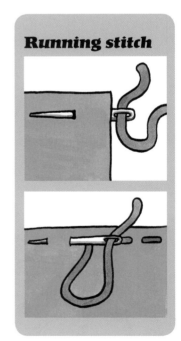

Running stitch

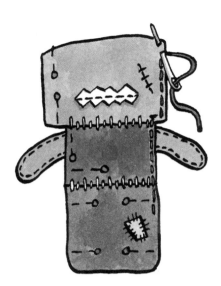

5 Place the front and back monster pieces wrong (back) sides together and insert the arms at each side. Pin and running stitch with black thread, leaving a gap along one side. Stuff, pin and sew up the gap. To finish, sew on the button eyes.

G - GHOST × 2 WHITE FELT

6 For the ghost softie, pin and cut out template G. Cut two small black felt circles for the eyes and a larger circle for the mouth. With a vanishing fabric pen, draw on the hands and backstitch over them with black thread. Sew on the mouth and eyes with small running stitches in white thread. Pin the front and back ghost pieces wrong sides together and running stitch around with black thread, leaving an opening along one side. Stuff and sew up the gap.

FuNKy FRuiT JuGGLiNG BaLLs

THESE FUN APPLE AND STRAWBERRY JUGGLING BALLS ARE QUICK TO MAKE AND ARE A GREAT WAY TO SHOW OFF YOUR SEWING SKILLS (AS WELL AS YOUR JUGGLING ABILITY)! WHY NOT TRY MAKING EACH SEGMENT IN A DIFFERENT FABRIC TO GIVE THE BALLS A COLOURFUL PATCHWORK EFFECT?

"Clipping and notching is important for curved shapes to make sure your fabric won't pull and pucker."

✏️ **What you will need** **FOR THE APPLES:** THREE DIFFERENT GREEN FABRICS 22 × 30CM (8½ × 12IN) • SCRAPS OF GREEN FELT • THREE BUTTONS • THREE 5MM (¼IN) GREEN WOODEN BEADS **FOR THE STRAWBERRIES:** • THREE DIFFERENT PINK OR RED FABRICS 22 × 30CM (8½ × 12IN) • SCRAPS OF GREEN FELT • SIX 5MM (¼IN) PINK WOODEN BEADS • 1.5KG (3¼LB) OF MILLET GRAIN, LENTILS OR RICE TO STUFF • TOPSTITCHING THREAD • FINE STRAW NEEDLE 6CM (2½IN) LONG • VANISHING FABRIC PEN • FUNNEL

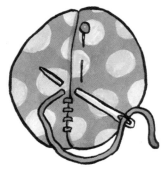

1 Cut out four of template A. Place template B in the centre of the wrong (back) side of each segment and draw on the stitching line and markers.

2 Place two segments right (front) sides together and backstitch one seam between the marks. Stitch the other segments right sides together to the unstitched seams of the first segments, then stitch them to each other, leaving a 5cm (2in) gap in the middle.

3 Cut across the point at the top and bottom of the ball then cut triangles out of the seams, taking care not to cut your stitches. This is called clipping and notching.

4 Turn through the gap, by pushing the ball inside out from wrong side to right side. Using a funnel, stuff firmly with millet grain, lentils or rice. Pin the gap closed and overstitch the seams together.

TRACE OR PHOTOCOPY THE TEMPLATES AND CUT OUT

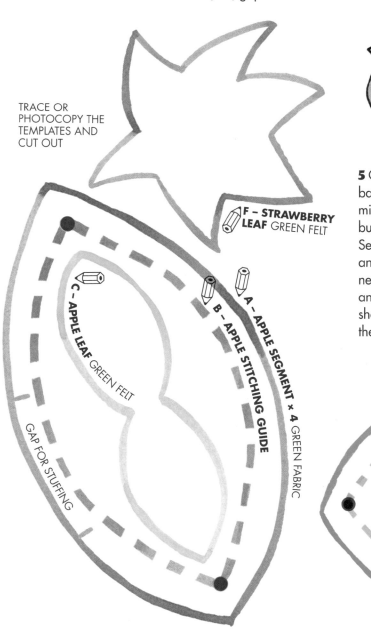

F – STRAWBERRY LEAF GREEN FELT

C – APPLE LEAF GREEN FELT

GAP FOR STUFFING

B – APPLE STITCHING GUIDE

A – APPLE SEGMENT × 4 GREEN FABRIC

5 Cut out template C and backstitch a line along the middle for the vein. Sew a button onto the base (see Sewing on a button). With an adult's help, push a needle through to the top and pull the thread tight to shape the apple. Stitch on the leaf and bead.

6 Push the needle back down to the base and wind the thread around the button a few times. Create a small stitch under the button, make a loop and push the needle through to create a knot. Repeat and cut off the remaining thread to finish.

D – STRAWBERRY SEGMENT × 4 PINK AND RED FABRIC

E – STRAWBERRY STITCHING GUIDE

7 For the strawberry juggling balls, follow Steps 1–6, using pink and red fabrics and green felt scraps and using templates D–F. Sew a bead to the base instead of a button.

GAP FOR STUFFING

exotic bird of paradise

WITH ITS BRIGHT COLOURS AND BEAUTIFULLY PATTERNED FABRICS, THIS DAZZLING BIRD OF PARADISE DECORATION IS SO EASY TO MAKE. IT WOULD MAKE A GREAT GIFT FOR A FRIEND OR WOULD LOOK REALLY EYE-CATCHING HANGING FROM A BEDROOM WINDOW.

"Add a little stuffing at a time and use a pencil to push it into narrow areas."

✏️ **What you will need** • BRIGHTLY COLOURED PATTERNED FABRIC 30CM (12IN) SQUARE • FUSIBLE INTERFACING 30CM (12IN) SQUARE • SCRAPS OF BRIGHTLY COLOURED FELT • EMBROIDERY THREAD • TOY STUFFING • RIBBON 36 × 0.5CM (14¼ × ¼IN) • EIGHT SMALL COLOURED FEATHERS • TWO SMALL BUTTONS • VANISHING FABRIC PEN • PENCIL

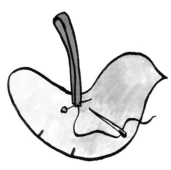

1 With an adult's help, press the fusible interfacing glue side down onto the wrong (back) side of the fabric. Using template A, pin and cut out two birds in a mirror image.

2 Use a vanishing fabric pen to mark the dot and gap marks on the wrong side of one of the bird pieces. Fold the ribbon in half, pin at the dot and secure with a few stitches.

3 Pin the wrong sides together and blanket stitch (see stitch panel) around the edges, leaving a gap between the two markers. Stuff the bird with toy stuffing and sew up the gap.

Blanket stitch

TRACE OR PHOTOCOPY THE TEMPLATES AND CUT OUT

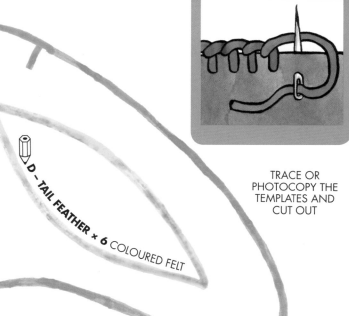

GAP FOR STUFFING

A – BIRD BODY × 2 (MIRROR IMAGE) PATTERNED FABRIC

STITCHING LINE

D – TAIL FEATHER × 6 COLOURED FELT

C – SMALL WING × 2 COLOURED FELT

B – LARGE WING × 2 COLOURED FELT

4 Cut out templates B and C in different coloured felts. Using the marked stitching line on the template, position shape B and overstitch in place. Add shape C and a small coloured feather on top and overstitch in place. Repeat on the other side.

5 For the tail, cut out six of template D. Sew on three felt feathers (see A) and three real feathers (see B) with a backstitch. Repeat on the other side. Sew on buttons for eyes.

A

B

Dazzling Yo-Yo Necklace

YO-YOS, ALSO KNOWN AS SUFFOLK PUFFS, ARE SIMPLE TO MAKE IN ANY SIZE. COMBINED WITH COLOURFUL FELT AND WOODEN BEADS AND STRUNG ONTO CORD, THEY CREATE A STRIKING NECKLACE DESIGN THAT WILL REALLY MAKE A STATEMENT!

What you will need • PRINTED COTTON FABRICS IN FIVE DIFFERENT COLOURS 15CM (6IN) SQUARE • FELT IN FIVE DIFFERENT COLOURS 10CM (4IN) SQUARE • WAXED COTTON CORD 1.2M (4FT) LENGTH • 16 SMALL WOODEN BEADS • ONE LARGE WOODEN BEAD APPROXIMATELY 1.5CM (⅝IN) IN DIAMETER • EMBROIDERY THREAD IN A SELECTION OF COLOURS • TOPSTITCHING THREAD

 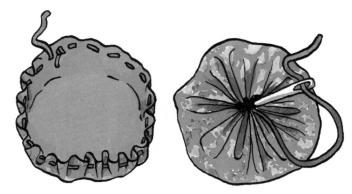 

1 Pin and cut out templates A–F onto fabric or felt as indicated. Take a fabric circle, thread a needle with topstitching thread and tie a double knot at one end. Running stitch 5mm (¼in) from the edge all the way around the circle.

2 Gently pull the thread back to the knotted end; the circle will gather up and fold over the edges. Even out the gathers. When the circle is fully gathered, lay on a flat surface and flatten the centre with your thumb. Your circle should now be half the size it started. Take the needle through to the back and secure the threads with a knot.

3 Lay the yo-yos onto the large felt circles and add a small felt circle at the centre. Thread a needle with embroidery thread and knot one end. From the back of the large felt circle, push the needle up through all the layers. Make a stitch across the middle, bringing the needle down to the back again. Repeat to make a cross stitch.

E – SMALL CIRCLE × 5 FELT

F – RECTANGLE × 5 FELT

4 Attach a small felt rectangle at the back of each yo-yo with an overstitch. Lay out the yo-yos and beads as desired and thread onto the cord. Knot the cord above the top beads and secure the yo-yos with overstiches.

5 Thread the large bead onto the top end of one cord and secure with a knot. Make a loop at the top end of the other cord and tie a knot. Wear and admire!

A – LARGE YO-YO COLOURED FABRIC

B – SMALL YO-YO × 4 COLOURED FABRIC

C – LARGE CIRCLE × 4 FELT

D – MEDIUM CIRCLE × 4 FELT

TRACE OR PHOTOCOPY THE TEMPLATES AND CUT OUT

"Try layering different size yo-yos on top of each other or adding buttons at the centres."

WISE OLD OWL

HAVE LOTS OF FUN MAKING
AND WEARING THIS
FANTASTIC OWL MASK.
MADE FROM FELT, IT IS SO
COMFORTABLE TO WEAR
AND THE FEATHERED FINISH
GIVES A DELIGHTFULLY
REALISTIC TOUCH.

✎ ***What you will need*** • FELT IN BROWN 22 × 50CM (8½ × 20IN), CREAM 12 × 22CM (4½ × 8½IN), STONE
10 × 23CM (4 × 9IN), ORANGE 8 × 16CM (3½ × 6¼IN) AND A SCRAP OF BLACK • BONDAWEB (DOUBLE-SIDED FUSIBLE
WEBBING) 20CM (8IN) • SELECTION OF BROWN/GREY SMALL FEATHERS • 3MM (⅛IN) BLACK ELASTIC 30CM (12IN) LENGTH
• EMBROIDERY THREAD IN DARK BROWN, CREAM, BURNT ORANGE AND BLACK • PENCIL • VANISHING FABRIC PEN

1 Cut out two of template A in brown felt. Draw templates B, C, D and E onto the smooth side of the Bondaweb and cut around each shape leaving a 5mm (¼in) border. With an adult's help, set an iron to hot and using a cloth to protect it, fuse the Bondaweb (rough side down) onto the reverse of the coloured felt. Now cut out the shapes on the pencil lines. Peel off the paper backing and place each shape, glue side down, on one of the brown felt head shapes (A) and ask an adult to press (iron) into position.

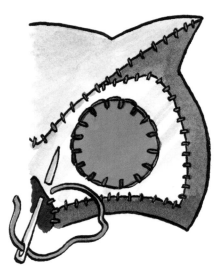

2 Blanket stitch in burnt orange thread around the outer edges of the orange eye surround (D). Straight stitch with cream thread around the cream middle of the head (C), with dark brown thread around the stone top of the head (B) and with black thread around the beak (E).

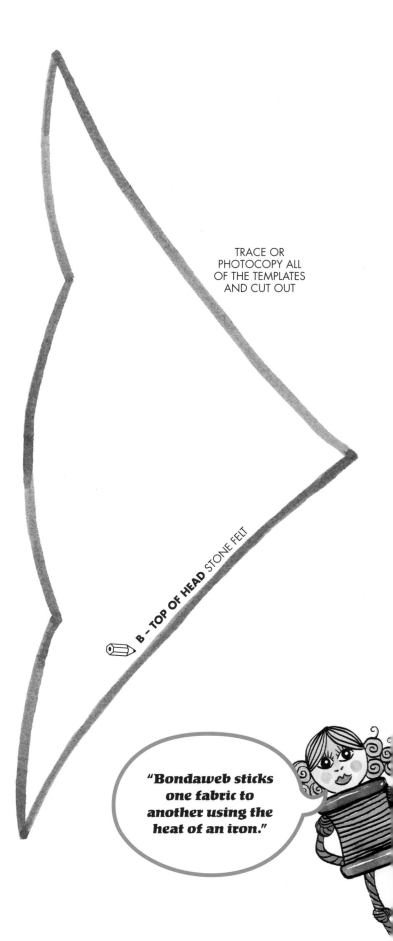

TRACE OR PHOTOCOPY ALL OF THE TEMPLATES AND CUT OUT

B – TOP OF HEAD STONE FELT

"Bondaweb sticks one fabric to another using the heat of an iron."

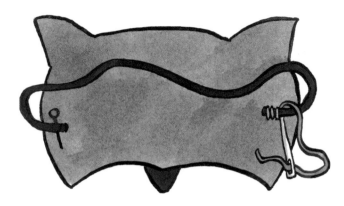

3 Hold the mask to your face and ask an adult to measure the elastic around the back of your head. Pin to the wrong side (back) of your mask and attach with an overstitch.

4 Take the remaining head (A) and pin to the wrong side of the decorated front. Take care not to trap the elastic inside. Blanket stitch the two layers together with dark brown thread.

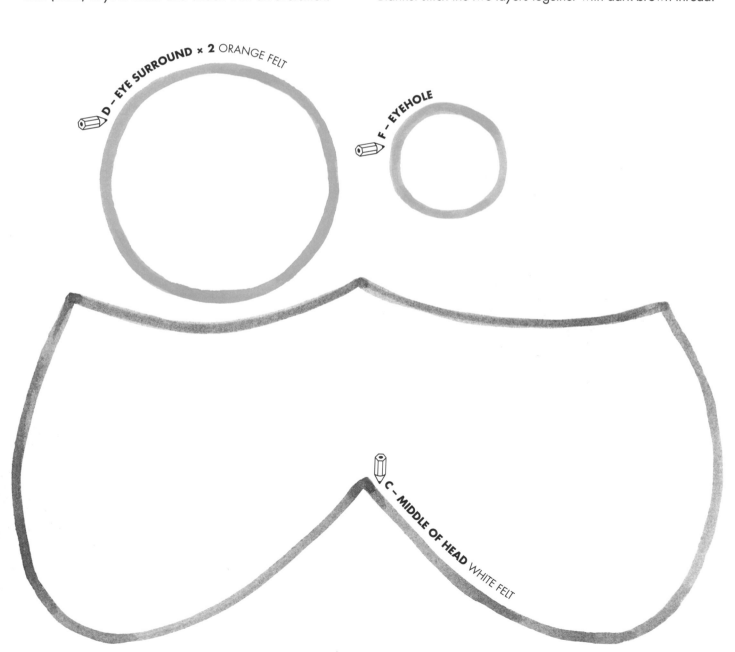

D – EYE SURROUND × 2 ORANGE FELT

F – EYEHOLE

C – MIDDLE OF HEAD WHITE FELT

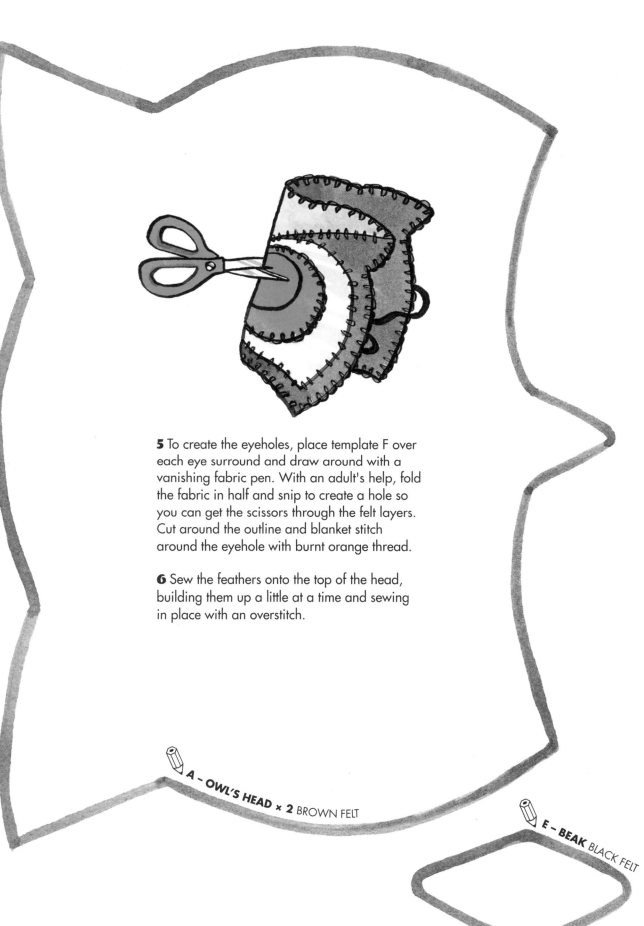

5 To create the eyeholes, place template F over each eye surround and draw around with a vanishing fabric pen. With an adult's help, fold the fabric in half and snip to create a hole so you can get the scissors through the felt layers. Cut around the outline and blanket stitch around the eyehole with burnt orange thread.

6 Sew the feathers onto the top of the head, building them up a little at a time and sewing in place with an overstitch.

A – OWL'S HEAD × 2 BROWN FELT

E – BEAK BLACK FELT

veggie Print cushion

BRIGHTEN UP YOUR BEDROOM BY PRINTING THIS UNIQUE FABRIC CUSHION WITH COLOURFUL SHAPES CUT FROM POTATOES OR OTHER VEGETABLES. EXPERIMENT BY CUTTING OUT DIFFERENT SHAPES OR EVEN PRINTING WITH OBJECTS SUCH AS BOTTLE TOPS OR CORKS.

✎ **What you will need** • MEDIUM WEIGHT CALICO 0.5 × 1.4M (20 × 56IN) • MEDIUM SIZED POTATO (OVAL SHAPED) • TWO CARROTS: MEDIUM AND LARGE SIZED • PATTERNED PAPER OR LINING PAPER • TOPSTITCHING THREAD (FOR HAND STITCHING) OR MULTIPURPOSE POLYESTER THREAD (FOR MACHINE STITCHING) • FABRIC PAINT IN PINK, YELLOW AND TURQUOISE, ONE POT OF EACH • PAINTBRUSH • SHARP KNIFE • VANISHING FABRIC PEN

1 Ask an adult to cut a potato in half using a sharp knife. To make shape A, draw two diagonal lines onto the potato using the rounded end to create the curve. Ask an adult to cut along the lines to a depth of about 5mm (¼in). Turn onto the side and cut 5mm (¼in) down to remove the excess potato.

2 Place shape B over the other half of the potato, draw around and cut out. With an adult's help, make a small and large circle shape by cutting across both carrots. Practise printing onto paper with your vegetable shapes.

3 On paper, draw and cut out a 44cm (17½in) square for the front and a 44 × 36cm (17½ × 14½in) rectangle for the back. Pin the front pattern onto the calico fabric and cut out. With a vanishing fabric pen, mark out a stitching line 2cm (¾in) in from the edge. Fold in half and quarter to find the centre point and lightly mark. Fold the remaining fabric in half, pin on the back pattern and cut out to make two pieces.

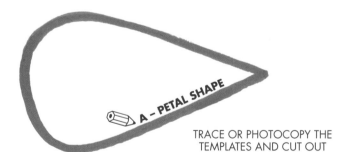

✏️ A – PETAL SHAPE

TRACE OR PHOTOCOPY THE TEMPLATES AND CUT OUT

4 Protect your table with newspaper and lay out the cushion front. Paint the point of potato shape A with yellow fabric paint and the rest of the shape with pink. Position onto the fabric with the point at the centre of the cushion. Press firmly and lift up. Print five more petals around the centre point, adding more paint each time.

"Mix the three fabric paints to create new colours: Yellow + Pink = Orange, Yellow + Turquoise = Green, Pink + Turquoise = Purple."

5 Mix a green colour and paint onto potato shape B. Following the illustration, print six leaves between the flower petals. Mix a purple colour, paint onto the small carrot circle and print a spot between each leaf. Paint shape A with pink paint and print twice at each corner inside the stitching line to create hearts.

6 Paint the large carrot shape with turquoise paint and print spots all over the cushion back. Paint the smaller carrot shape with mixed orange paint and print smaller spots between the larger ones. Leave to dry and ask an adult to press (iron) the fabric on the reverse side to fix the paint.

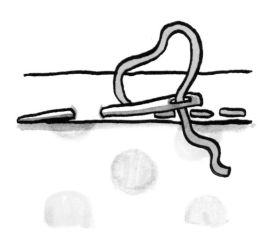

7 Take the two back cushion pieces and with an adult's help, press the top longest edges over by 2cm (¾in) then a further 2cm (¾in). Pin, then running stitch the edge down to make a hem.

8 With the front cushion piece facing up, place one of the back pieces over it with right (front) sides together. Place the second back piece on top, positioning the stitched hems to the middle and the raw edges to the outside. Pin and stitch around the outside, 2cm (¾in) from the edge on the stitching line. Trim the corners, turn through and ask an adult to press.

"Paint a thin even covering of fabric paint onto your shapes, press down flat firmly and lift up carefully."

B – LEAF SHAPE

TRACE OR PHOTOCOPY THE
TEMPLATES AND CUT OUT

catch a falling starfish

THIS SPARKLING STARFISH DREAMCATCHER CAN BE HUNG IN YOUR BEDROOM WINDOW TO CATCH THE SUN'S RAYS AND BRING YOU HAPPY DREAMS OF SAND AND SEA. THE BEADS AND SEQUINS GLITTER BEAUTIFULLY AS THEY CATCH THE LIGHT.

✎ **What you will need** • 2M (6½FT) SILVER RIBBON 5MM (¼IN) WIDTH • FELT IN ORANGE 20 × 40CM (8 × 16IN) AND IN TURQUOISE, PURPLE, PEA GREEN AND BLUE, EACH PIECE 20CM (8IN) SQUARED• 30CM (12IN) EMBROIDERY HOOP • 2M (6½FT) TURQUOISE BIAS BINDING • 2M (6½FT) TURQUOISE POMPOM TRIMMING • SEQUINS IN VARIOUS SIZES AND COLOURS • SELECTION OF COLOURED RIBBONS AND TRIMS 5MM (¼IN) WIDTH • BLACK WAXED COTTON CORD 1.3M (4¼FT) LENGTH • EMBROIDERY THREAD IN ORANGE, TURQUOISE, PURPLE, GREEN AND BLUE • SELECTION OF LARGE HOLED GLASS BEADS • TOY STUFFING • LARGE CHENILLE NEEDLE • GENERAL SEWING NEEDLE

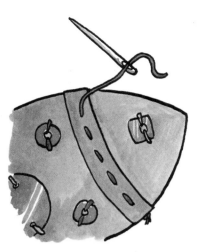

1 Unscrew the embroidery hoop and separate the outer and inner hoops. You will be using the inner (solid) hoop only. Wind the bias binding around the hoop, covering up the wood. Cut off the excess, fold the end under and secure with an overstitch. Loosely wind the pom pom trimming over the top.

2 Pin and cut out templates A and B in the felt colours indicated. Transfer the markings.

3 Stitch sequins onto the starfish, sewing from the centre outwards to the points. Thread a general sewing needle with sewing thread, tie a knot in the end and sew on the sequins (see stitch panel). If the sequin has two holes, repeat on the opposite side. Sew sequins on the fish and attach ribbon and trims with running stitch.

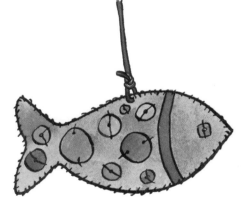

Sewing sequins

4 Select matching embroidery thread, split it in half (into three threads) and sew around the fish and starfish with a small overstitch, leaving a gap between the markers. Lightly stuff, pushing the stuffing into all the points and overstitch the gap closed.

5 Cut the waxed cord into three 35cm (14in) lengths and thread one length onto the chenille needle. With an adult's help, push the needle through the top of a fish at the marker then tie a knot and cut off the short end.

"Make this as a mobile using an alternative design - butterflies would look great!"

6 Tie another knot about 3cm (1¼in) from the first and thread on five beads. Tie a knot above them to secure then tie the end of the cord to the ring with a double knot. Repeat with the other cords. To add the second fish on the central string, you will need to push the needle all the way through the first fish.

7 For the starfish, take the remaining piece of cord and attach from a point in the same way. Add three large beads and tie a double knot at the hoop, close to the top bead.

A – FISH × 2 EACH OF TURQUOISE, PURPLE, PEA GREEN AND BLUE FELT

TRACE OR PHOTOCOPY BOTH TEMPLATES AND CUT OUT

B – STARFISH × 2 ORANGE FELT

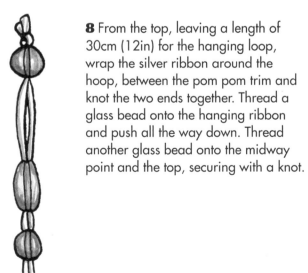

8 From the top, leaving a length of 30cm (12in) for the hanging loop, wrap the silver ribbon around the hoop, between the pom pom trim and knot the two ends together. Thread a glass bead onto the hanging ribbon and push all the way down. Thread another glass bead onto the midway point and the top, securing with a knot.

"To thread a bead onto frayed ribbon, wrap sticky tape around the end, making it firm enough to thread the bead through. It can be cut off afterwards."

sleepy cat case

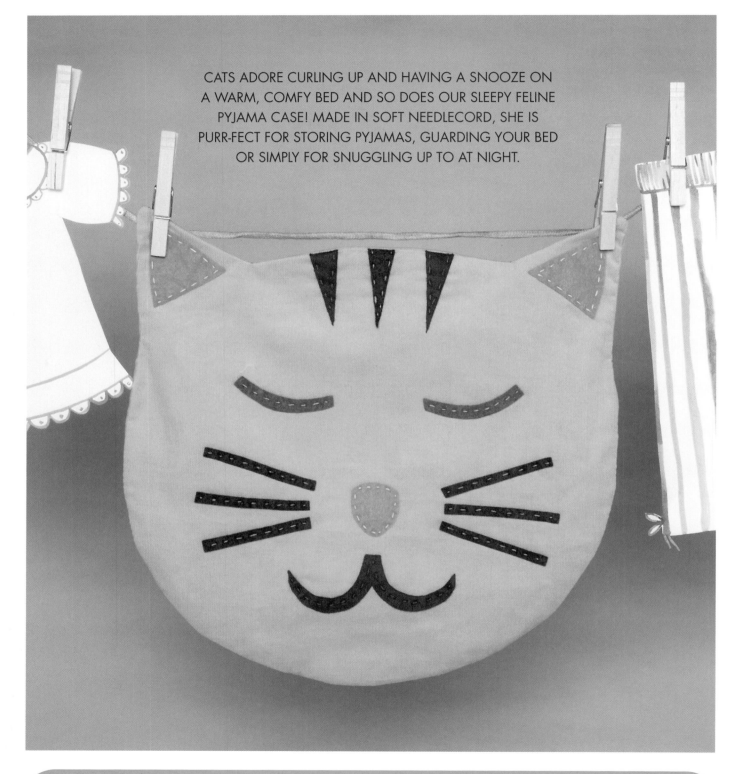

CATS ADORE CURLING UP AND HAVING A SNOOZE ON A WARM, COMFY BED AND SO DOES OUR SLEEPY FELINE PYJAMA CASE! MADE IN SOFT NEEDLECORD, SHE IS PURR-FECT FOR STORING PYJAMAS, GUARDING YOUR BED OR SIMPLY FOR SNUGGLING UP TO AT NIGHT.

✎ *What you will need*
• NEEDLECORD COTTON FABRIC 50 × 90CM (20 × 36IN) • SCRAPS OF FELT IN PURPLE, PINK, BROWN AND OLIVE • BONDAWEB (DOUBLE-SIDED FUSIBLE WEBBING) • 30CM (12IN) ZIP • TOPSTITCHING THREAD (FOR HANDSTITCHING) OR POLYESTER MULTIPURPOSE THREAD (FOR MACHINE STITCHING) • EMBROIDERY THREADS • VANISHING FABRIC PEN • PENCIL • PAPER

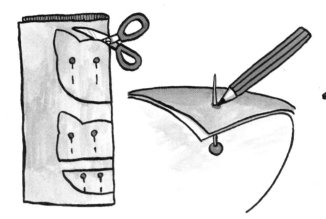

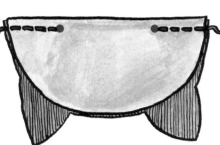

1 With an adult's help, press (iron) the needlecord fabric and fold it in half. Lay the straight edge of templates A, B and C on the folded edge, pin and cut out. Transfer the dots onto the two back pieces of your fabric by putting a pin through each one.

2 Place the back top and bottom pieces (templates B and C) right (front) sides together and line up along the straight edge. Backstitch a 2cm (¾in) seam, leaving a gap between the two dots on the straight edge. Press the seam open.

PLACE ON FOLDLINE

TRACE OR PHOTOCOPY ALL OF THE TEMPLATES AND CUT OUT

D – EAR × 2 PINK FELT

C – **BACK** COTTON FABRIC

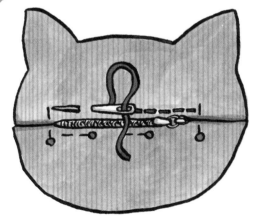

3 With the zip facing up, place under the gap and line up one edge to the teeth. Pin along the line, securing each end. Line up the other edge to meet the first and pin as before. Opening the zip makes it easier for you to pin. Sew in place with running stitch using embroidery thread.

"To make a stuffed cushion, cut the front and back fabric in the same shape, omit the zip and leave a gap to turn through before stuffing."

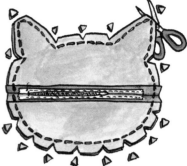

4 Trace templates D, E, F, G, H and I onto the paper (smooth) side of the Bondaweb. Cut around each shape leaving a 5mm (¼in) border. Place onto the felt, cover with a cloth and press with an adult's help. Leave to cool and cut out the shapes on the pencil lines.

5 Peel off the paper backing and position the shapes onto the right side of the front cat fabric. Cover with a cloth and press in place (smaller shapes may need to be pinned). Running stitch the felt shapes to the fabric using matching embroidery thread.

6 Draw a stitching line 1cm (⅜in) in from the edge on the wrong (back) side of the back piece. Open the zip and with right sides together, pin the front and back of the cat around the edge. Sew on the stitching line with backstitch or on the sewing machine. Trim back and clip the curved edges then turn through and press.

A – **FRONT** COTTON FABRIC

H – WHISKERS × 6 PURPLE FELT

PLACE ON FOLDLINE

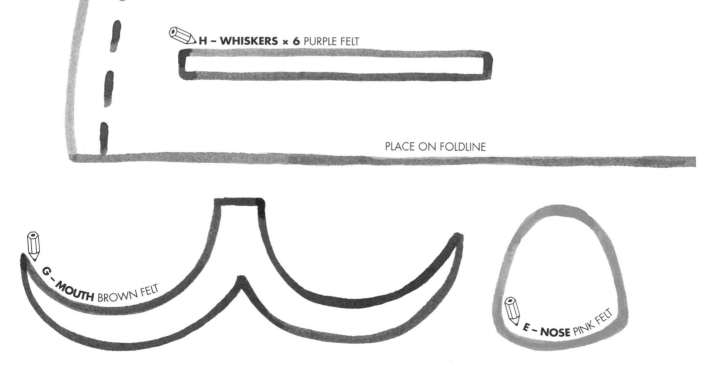

G – **MOUTH** BROWN FELT

E – **NOSE** PINK FELT

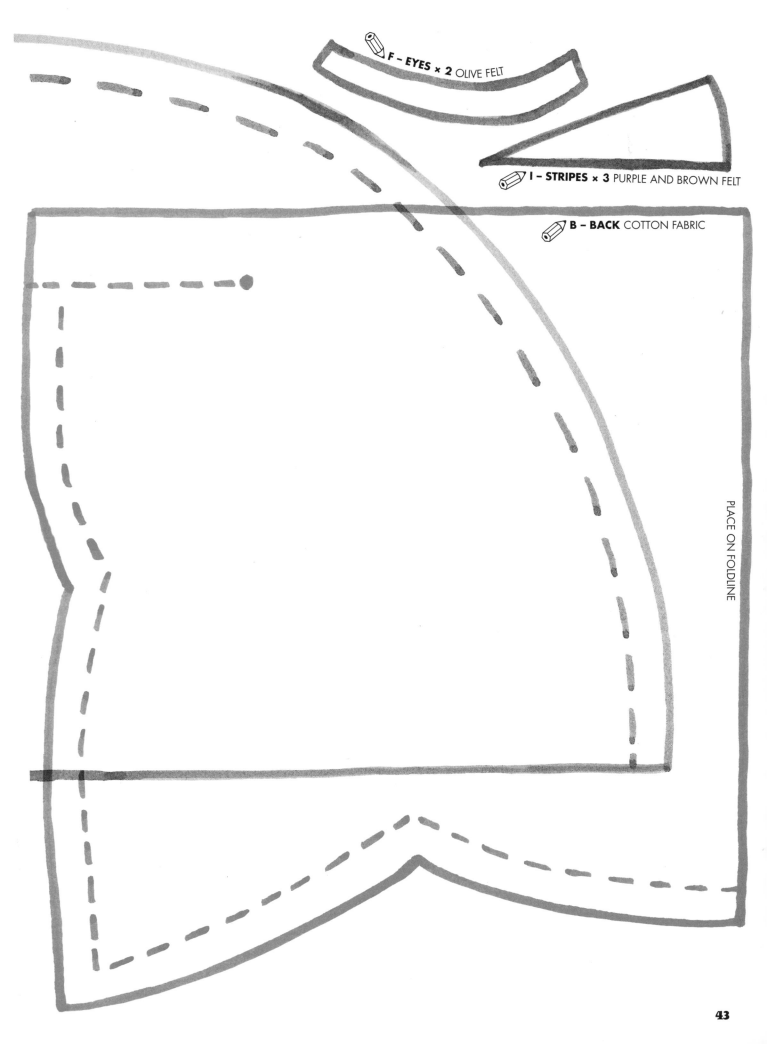

F – EYES × 2 OLIVE FELT

I – STRIPES × 3 PURPLE AND BROWN FELT

B – BACK COTTON FABRIC

PLACE ON FOLDLINE

SPRINGTIME BUNNIES

THIS SWEET PICTURE SHOWING TWO PLAYFUL RABBITS IN THE SPRING IS THE PERFECT INTRODUCTION TO NEEDLECRAFT, AS IT CONTAINS EIGHT OF THE ESSENTIAL STITCHES THAT YOU NEED TO START EMBROIDERING. USE AS FEW OR AS MANY AS YOU DESIRE!

What you will need • 30CM (12IN) EMBROIDERY HOOP • 28–COUNT LINEN 40 × 70CM (16 × 28IN) (EXTRA ALLOWED FOR PRACTISING) • EMBROIDERY THREAD IN DARK BROWN, BROWN, PINK, WHITE, GREY, YELLOW, LIGHT GREEN, MID GREEN AND GRASS GREEN • EMBROIDERY NEEDLE • PENCIL • PENCIL OR VANISHING FABRIC PEN

1 Cut a 40cm (16in) square of linen and tape it down over the drawing to prevent it from moving. The image will be visible beneath the linen, allowing you to retrace it with either a pencil or vanishing fabric pen.

2 Open up the embroidery hoop and put the solid ring underneath the linen and the ring with the screw on the top. Push the two rings together with the screw at the top of the design, making sure that the linen is taut. With an adult's help, firmly tighten the screw.

3 Cut a length of embroidery thread to around 60cm (24in) (any longer and it will knot or tangle) and thread onto the needle. Push the needle through to the front, leaving a 1cm (⅜in) end at the back. Hold the end down with your thumb and make two tiny stitches to secure the threads – the loose ends can be cut off afterwards. Hold the hoop in your left hand if you are right-handed or your right hand if left-handed and work from the front.

4 The eight embroidery stitches (see also Stitch Library) used are as follows:
• The outline circle and branches are sewn in **running stitch**: work from right to left, taking the needle in and out of the fabric and pulling the thread through. Keep your stitches small and evenly spaced.
• The rabbits are sewn in **backstitch**: bring the needle up to the front of the design. Take a backward stitch and then bring the needle up a little way ahead of the first stitch. Insert the needle into the point where the first stitch finished.

• The long grass and grass in the foreground are sewn in **stem (outline) stitch**: working from left to right, bring the needle up to the front and make a stitch. Bring the needle back up halfway along the first stitch to the left side and make another stitch. Continue with small, even stitches.

"Using an embroidery hoop keeps your linen flat, making it easier to sew neat, even stitches"

• The tree trunk is sewn in **chain stitch**: bring the thread out and hold down with your thumb. Insert the needle next to where it last emerged and bring the point out a little way in front. Pull through, keeping the thread under the needlepoint to form a looped stitch.

• The leaves and flowers are sewn in **detached chain stitch**: work in the same way as chain stitch but fasten over each loop with a small stitch. To make the daisies, work around in a group to create flower petals – this is known as **lazy daisy stitch**.
• The blossom and flower centres are sewn with **French knots**: bring the needle to the front and hold the thread down. Twist the thread around the needle two or three times. Insert the needle close to where the thread emerged and pull tightly through, creating a neat knot on the surface.

• The eyes are sewn with **satin stitch**: following the outline, bring the needle to the front on one side and take the stitch over to the other side. Continue, keeping the stitches close and the edges even.
• The short grass is sewn with **long (straight) stitch**: worked like a single running stitch, vary the length to create long or short stitches.

5 As you sew, keep pulling the needle up to release the thread or you will start sewing a double thickness. To join on a new thread, finish off the stitch by pushing the needle through to the back of the work and sewing two small stitches. As you pull the thread through on the last stitch, push the needle through the loop to create a knot and cut off threads. Start a new thread (see Step 3).

6 When your embroidery is complete, with an adult's help, check that the screw is still firmly secured and carefully cut off the excess linen around the edge of the hoop.

TRACE OR PHOTOCOPY
THE OUTLINE DRAWING

47

BOYS VERSUS GIRLS

BOYS VERSUS GIRLS IS A FUN INTERPRETATION OF THE TRADITIONAL NOUGHTS AND CROSSES GAME, MADE MORE EXCITING BY USING CHILDREN'S FACES AS COUNTERS. YOU WILL ENJOY DESIGNING THE CHARACTER COUNTERS AS MUCH PLAYING THE GAME ITSELF!

✎ **What you will need** • GREEN FLORAL COTTON FABRIC 50CM (20IN) SQUARE • BLUE FELT 45CM (18IN) SQUARE • TEN PIECES OF FELT (FOR FACES) IN A SELECTION OF DARK BROWN, MID BROWN, PALE PINK AND CREAM, EACH PIECE 15 × 30CM (6 × 12IN) • TEN PIECES OF FELT (FOR HAIR) IN A SELECTION OF BLACK, GOLD, BROWN AND YELLOW, EACH PIECE 15 × 20CM (6 × 8IN) • COLOURED FELT SCRAPS (FOR HAIR BOWS) • 1.5CM (⅝IN) WIDE BLACK RIBBON, FOUR 50CM (20IN) LENGTHS • PATTERN PAPER 60CM (24IN) SQUARE • SELECTION OF MATCHING EMBROIDERY THREADS • EMBROIDERY THREAD (FOR HAND STITCHING) OR POLYESTER MULTIPURPOSE THREAD (FOR MACHINE SEWING) IN BLACK AND BLUE • VANISHING FABRIC PEN • PENCIL • RULER

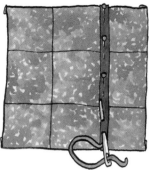

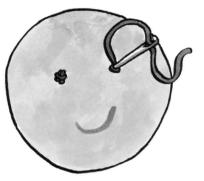

1 On plain paper, draw a 49cm (19½in) square in pencil and cut out. Pin onto the green floral fabric and cut out. With an adult's help, press (iron) each edge over 2cm (¾in) to the wrong (back) side.

2 On the right side (front), measure and mark 15cm (6in) intervals along each side. Draw in the lines with a vanishing fabric pen. Lay the black ribbon over the marked lines. Pin and running stitch in black embroidery thread or sew using polyester multipurpose thread on a sewing machine.

3 Draw a 45cm (18in) square onto the blue felt and cut out. Place the green top fabric over the felt square and pin together. Running stitch along the four edges.

4 Cut out template A in flesh-coloured felt. You will need two circles of the same colour for each face (ten pairs in total). Cut out one felt hair shape for each of the five boys and five girls in various colours using templates B–K.

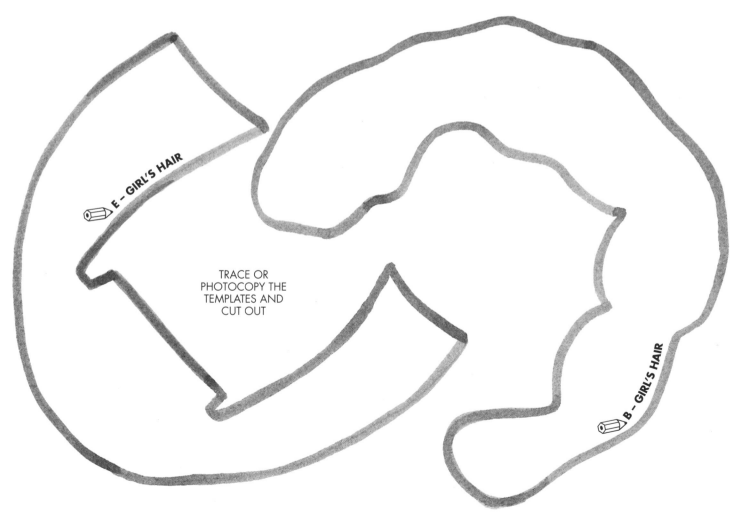

E – GIRL'S HAIR

B – GIRL'S HAIR

TRACE OR PHOTOCOPY THE TEMPLATES AND CUT OUT

H – BOY'S HAIR

M – LARGE HAIR BOW

A – CIRCLE × 10 PAIRS

5 Place the hair onto your felt circles to help you position your features. Lightly draw in the eyes, mouth, glasses and freckles using a vanishing fabric pen. Sew with backstitch for the mouth and with overstitch or backstitch for the eyes. Pin the completed face on top of the second circle in the same colour and running stitch together. Pin the hair onto the face and sew the hairline with running stitch. Turn over and continue to stitch from the back around the outer circle.

"This two-player game has the same rules as noughts and crosses: one person plays with the girl's team and the other the boy's team."

I – BOY'S HAIR

K – BOY'S HAIR

F – GIRL'S HAIR

G – BOY'S HAIR

L – SMALL HAIR BOW

C – GIRL'S HAIR

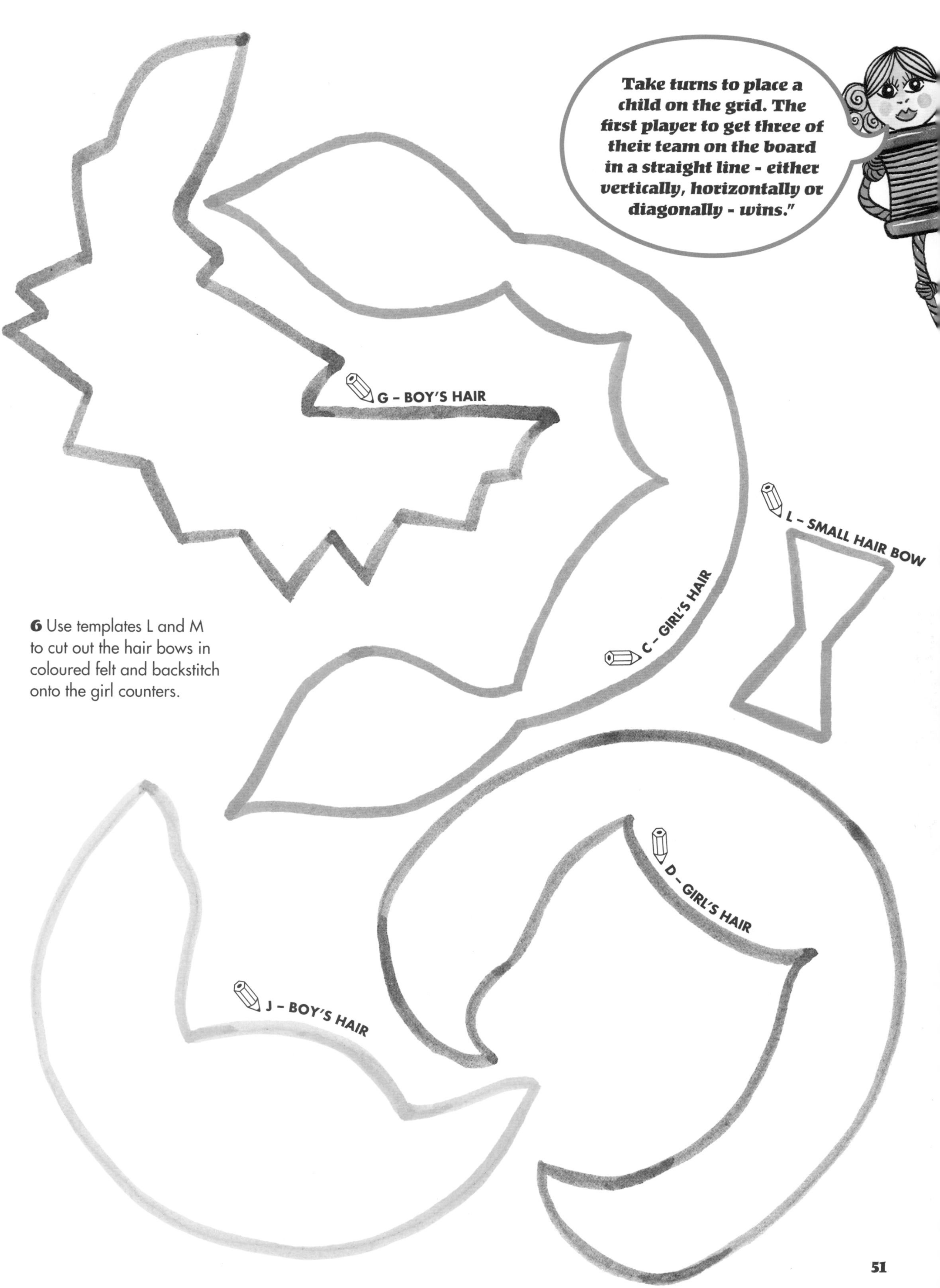

6 Use templates L and M to cut out the hair bows in coloured felt and backstitch onto the girl counters.

D – GIRL'S HAIR

J – BOY'S HAIR

Take turns to place a child on the grid. The first player to get three of their team on the board in a straight line - either vertically, horizontally or diagonally - wins."

Pentagon Patchwork Ball

THIS BRIGHT AND BOLD BALL IS MADE ENTIRELY WITH PENTAGONS USING A CLEVER TECHNIQUE KNOWN AS ENGLISH PAPER PIECING. FABRIC IS SIMPLY WRAPPED OVER PAPER TEMPLATES TO CREATE THE SHAPES THAT ARE THEN HAND SEWN TOGETHER FOR FANTASTIC RESULTS.

✎ **What you will need** • PRINTED PLAIN COTTON FABRIC 15 × 45CM (6 × 18IN) • CHECKED COTTON FABRIC 15 × 45CM (6 × 18IN) • PLAIN STRIPED COTTON FABRIC 15 × 45CM (6 × 18IN) • MULTI-COLOURED STRIPED FABRIC 15 × 45CM (6 × 18IN) • THREE SHEETS OF FREEZER PAPER OR A4 COPY PAPER • TOY STUFFING • COTTON THREAD (FOR TACKING) • TOPSTITCHING THREAD (FOR SEWING)

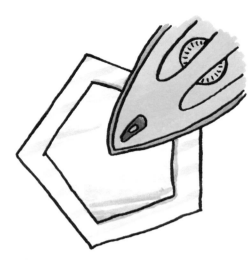

"Freezer paper has a waxy finish on one side that sticks to fabric when ironed down and can be easily removed."

1 Using template A, pin and cut out three pentagons of each fabric (twelve in total). Using template B, draw twelve pentagons onto the paper (non waxy) side of freezer paper or onto copy paper. With an adult's help, press (iron) the waxy side of template B centrally onto the wrong (back) side of the fabric. If using copy paper, pin template B.

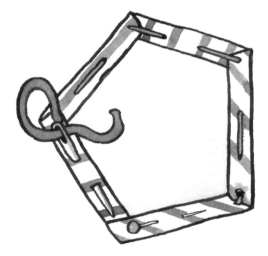

2 Fold and pin the fabric edges over the template and in a contrasting cotton thread, tack (baste) all the way around, holding down each corner with a stitch. Tacking (basting) is a long running stitch that holds fabric in place before properly sewing and can be pulled out afterwards.

3 To make sure that your colours are balanced and fabrics are not repeated next to each other, follow the illustration above.

Overstich

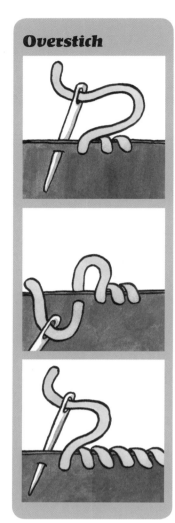

4 Thread your needle with topstitching thread. Taking pentagons 1 and 2, put right (front) sides of the fabric together and overstitch (see stitch panel) along one edge. Join pieces 1–3, 1–4, 1–5 and 1–6 and repeat with pieces 7–8, 7–9, 7–10, 7–11 and 7–12.

5 Referring to Step 3 illustration, stitch pieces 6–8, then join up all the side edges with an overstitch so that the ball begins to take shape. Sew around all the sides, leaving just one side open.

TRACE OR PHOTOCOPY THE TEMPLATES AND CUT OUT

"To create a ball shape you must use pentagons - they will always curve when sewn together."

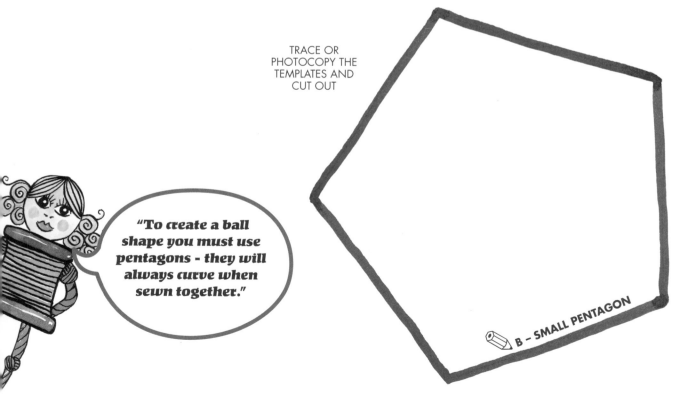

B – SMALL PENTAGON

6 Remove all of your tacking stitches and carefully pull out the paper templates. Turn the ball to the right side through the opening and stuff firmly with toy stuffing. Sew up the opening with a small neat overstitch.

A – LARGE PENTAGON

Hippy Handbag

A FAVOURITE PATTERNED FABRIC INSPIRED THIS EASY-TO-MAKE, FUNKY HANDBAG. THE PAISLEY SHAPES INFLUENCED THE SIMPLE RUNNING STITCH BACKGROUND EMBROIDERY AND WE ADDED SOME FABULOUS COLOURFUL YARN FLOWERS TO GIVE THE BAG MORE DIMENSION.

What you will need • BRIGHTLY PATTERNED COTTON LINING FABRIC 0.5 × 1M (20 × 40IN) • FELT IN SPICE OR ANOTHER COLOUR TO MATCH YOUR FABRIC 0.5 × 1M (20 × 40IN) • TAPESTRY OR FOUR-PLY YARN IN FIVE MATCHING COLOURS 3M (9¾FT) • CHUNKY WOOL IN SIX MATCHING COLOURS 1.3M (4¼FT) • SELECTION OF MATCHING EMBROIDERY THREADS • EMBROIDERY NEEDLE • TAPESTRY NEEDLE • VANISHING FABRIC PEN • PENCIL • PAPER • STIFF CARDBOARD

1 Fold the printed lining fabric in half, pin on Template A and cut out. With an adult's help, press over both top edges to the wrong side by 1cm (³⁄₈in). To cut the main bag, trim the paper pattern along the dotted line and cut out two in spice felt.

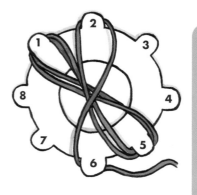

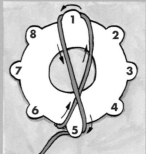

2 Using template B, draw six paisley shapes onto both felt pieces with a vanishing fabric pen. Using a different embroidery thread for each paisley, secure with a small backstitch or knot on the wrong (back) side then running stitch along the marked lines. Stitch a second row inside the first.

3 Trace template C onto stiff card and ask an adult to cut out. Cut 2m (6½ft) of yarn and tape one end to the back next to spoke (5). Bring the yarn up and anticlockwise around the opposite spoke (1). Bring it down to the starting spoke (5) and wind clockwise around (see stitch panel). Repeat to create a petal. Work clockwise around the loom, winding opposite spokes in a figure of eight. Thread the yarn end onto a blunt tapestry needle, stitch through the centre to the back and trim off, leaving about 6cm (2½in).

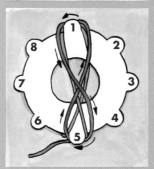

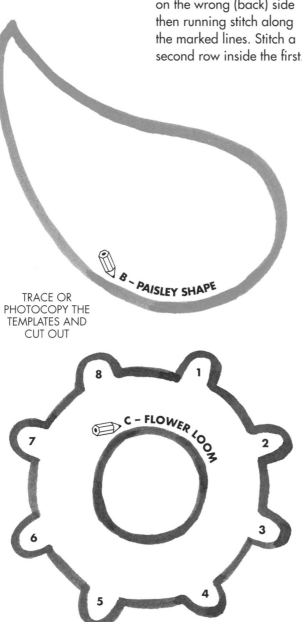

B – PAISLEY SHAPE

TRACE OR PHOTOCOPY THE TEMPLATES AND CUT OUT

C – FLOWER LOOM

"For fuller flowers, try a thicker yarn. The centres can be stitched around twice."

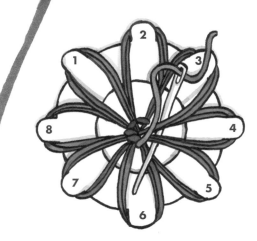

5 Position the yarn flowers onto the felt, at least 2cm (¾in) away from the sides. Hold or pin the flowers on the front and overstitch onto the felt from the back with embroidery thread. Repeat on the back.

4 For the backstitch centre, thread an embroidery needle with a contrast thread and knot at the back. Bring the needle up between spokes (8) and (1). Take the thread over two petals (to the right) inserting the needle between petals (7) and (6). Bring back up between petals (7) and (8) then continue around the flower. Secure with a few stitches at the back, tie off any loose threads and trim then remove from the loom. Repeat to make as many flowers as you wish.

6 To sew the bag, place the two felt pieces right (front) sides together and pin along the curved edge. Draw a stitchline 1cm (⅜in) away from the outside edge and hand sew with backstitch or machine sew with straight stitch. Repeat with the fabric pieces. Use scissors to clip the curves of the felt only and turn through to the right side.

TRACE OR PHOTOCOPY THE TEMPLATES AND CUT OUT

7 Insert the stitched fabric lining into the felt bag, match up the side seams and pin together along the top edge. Running stitch together with a contrasting embroidery thread.

8 For the handle, take six strands of coloured wool and knot at one end. Tape the end to a table and separate into three. Plait together and knot then trim the end. Pin to the outside of the bag at the side seams and secure with four or five large overstitches above and below the knots.

A – HANDBAG × **2** IN FELT AND × **2** IN COTTON LINING FABRIC

DRESS UP DOLLS

INSPIRED BY OUR CHILDHOOD LOVE OF PAPER DRESS UP DOLLS, WE CREATED THESE FUN FELT DOLLS WITH PIRATE AND FAIRY COSTUMES. USE OUR TEMPLATES OR GET CREATIVE AND DESIGN A WHOLE NEW WARDROBE FOR YOUR FELT FRIENDS.

✎ **What you will need** FOR EACH DOLL: FLESH COLOURED FELT 28 × 40CM (11 × 16IN) • FUSIBLE WADDING (BATTING) 28 × 40CM (11 × 16IN) • BACKING FELT 28 × 40CM (11 × 16IN) **YOU WILL ALSO NEED:** FELT FOR HAIR • SELECTION OF FABRICS AND FELT FOR CLOTHING • BONDAWEB (DOUBLE-SIDED FUSIBLE WEBBING), 1M (40IN) • FLESH COLOURED EMBROIDERY THREAD • SELECTION OF EMBROIDERY THREADS FOR STITCHING CLOTHES AND FEATURES • 3 BUTTONS (FOR GIRL'S BLOUSE) • NARROW GOLD RIBBON (FOR FAIRY DRESS) 36CM (14¼IN) • NARROW PINK RIBBON 15CM (6IN) • WHITE ROUGH SEW-ON VELCRO OR VELCRO DOTS • VANISHING FABRIC PEN • PENCIL

1 With an adult's help and a pressing cloth, press (iron) the fusible wadding on the reverse of the flesh felt and lay template A on top. Draw around with a vanishing fabric pen, remove the template and cut out. Then cut one of A in the backing felt.

2 Lay templates B and D (girl) or M (boy) onto felt, draw around using a vanishing fabric pen and cut out.

"Embroidery thread is made from six strands of cotton. Split it in half (three strands) to make it easier to sew with."

3 Using a pencil, trace the briefs templates C (girl) or L (boy) onto the paper (smooth) side of the Bondaweb. Roughly cut out with a small border around each shape – do not cut on the pencil lines. Place the Bondaweb glue (rough) side down onto the back of your fabric, cover with a cloth and with an adult's help, press with a hot iron. Wait for the paper to cool then cut out on the pencil lines. Peel off the paper and position the briefs glue side down onto the doll, cover with a cloth and press into place.

C – BRIEFS (GIRL) *FABRIC*

K – SHOES *FELT*

E – BLOUSE *FABRIC*

TRACE OR PHOTOCOPY ALL OF THE TEMPLATES AND CUT OUT

4 Position the boy's or girl's felt hair and vest (girl doll only) onto the doll front. Sew these and the briefs with running stitch. Draw on the features with a vanishing fabric pen. Sew the eyes with an overstitch and the mouth with backstitch.

5 Place the doll front and backing felt wrong (back) sides together. Pin and overstitch together.

6 To make the felt clothes draw around the templates and cut out in felt (see Step 2). For the fabric clothes use the Bondaweb process (see Step 3) but press the cut out fabric garments onto white felt, trim back the excess felt and secure with running stitch. Add details with stitches, buttons, felt shapes and sequins. To stick the clothes to the felt doll, sew small squares of rough Velcro onto the reverse of each garment or apply small stick-on Velcro dots.

🖉 **P – POCKET** FELT

🖉 **M – HAIR** FELT

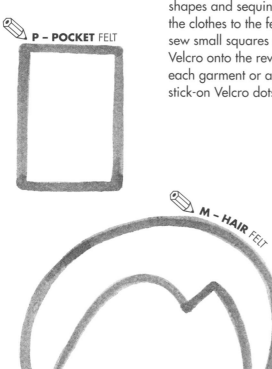

🖉 **O – DUNGAREES** FELT

7 Decorate the clothing as follows:

Fairy wings Draw two wings onto white felt using template I and cut out. Pin and running stitch the two wings together. Sew sparkly sequins onto the outer edges of the wings.

Fairy dress Cut ribbon into three 12cm (4¾in) lengths. Pin it on, following the dotted lines on template J. Running stitch over the ribbon and around the edges of the dress.

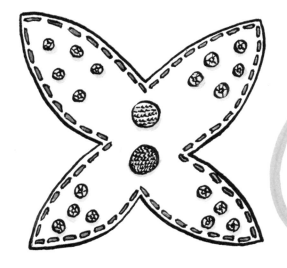

D – HAIR FELT

I – FAIRY WINGS WHITE FELT

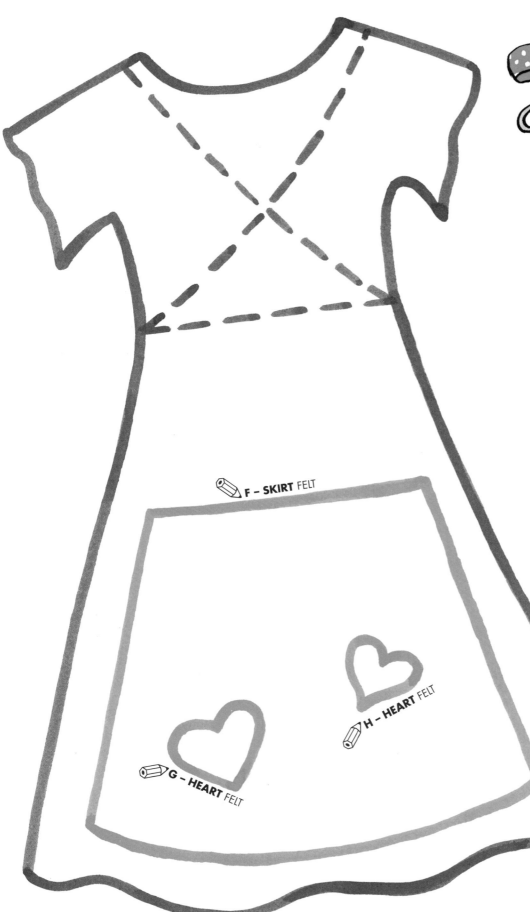

F – SKIRT FELT

H – HEART FELT

G – HEART FELT

J – FAIRY DRESS FABRIC

Girl doll's hair bow
Cut pink ribbon to a length of 5.5cm (2¼in). Fold 1.5cm (⅝in) in at each end towards the back and secure with a stitch. Fold a 4.5cm (1¾in) ribbon over the centre to make a band and secure with a few stitches. Sew on a piece of rough (male) Velcro.

Girl's skirt Cut out heart templates G and H in red felt. Pin onto a pink felt skirt and overstitch into place.

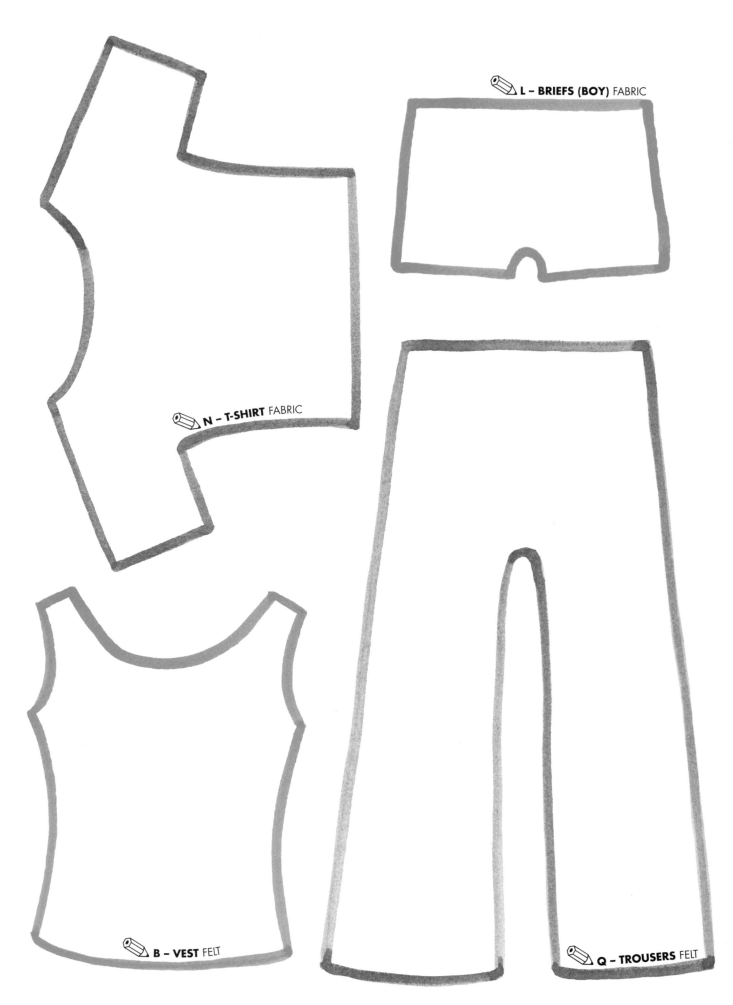

L – **BRIEFS (BOY)** FABRIC

N – **T-SHIRT** FABRIC

B – **VEST** FELT

Q – **TROUSERS** FELT

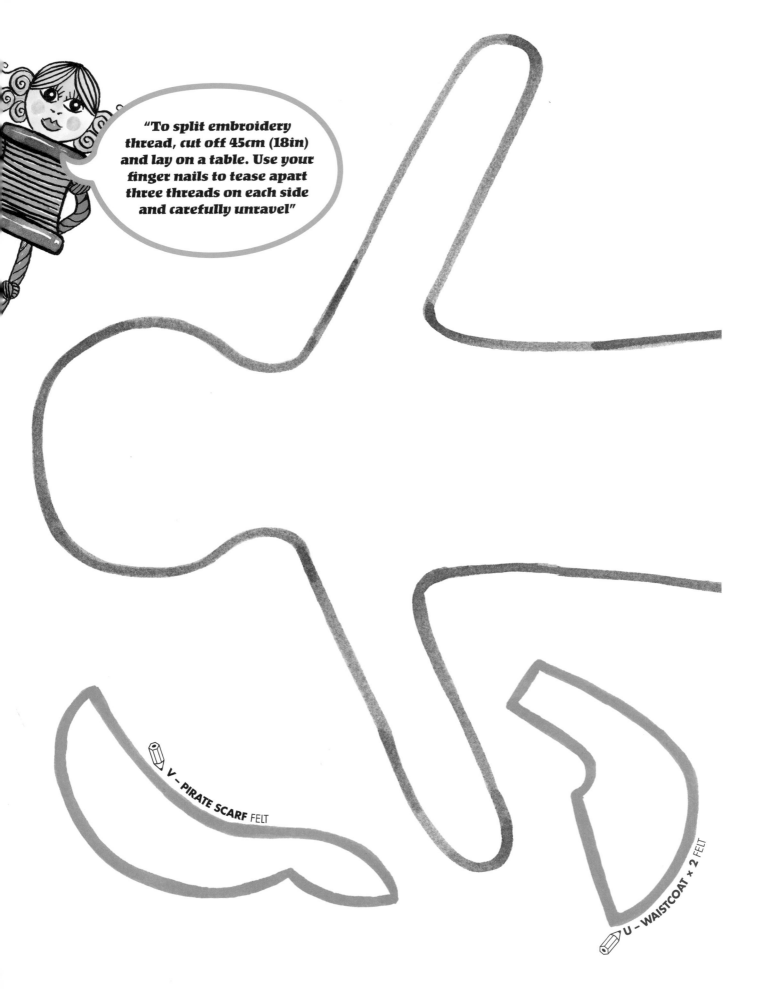

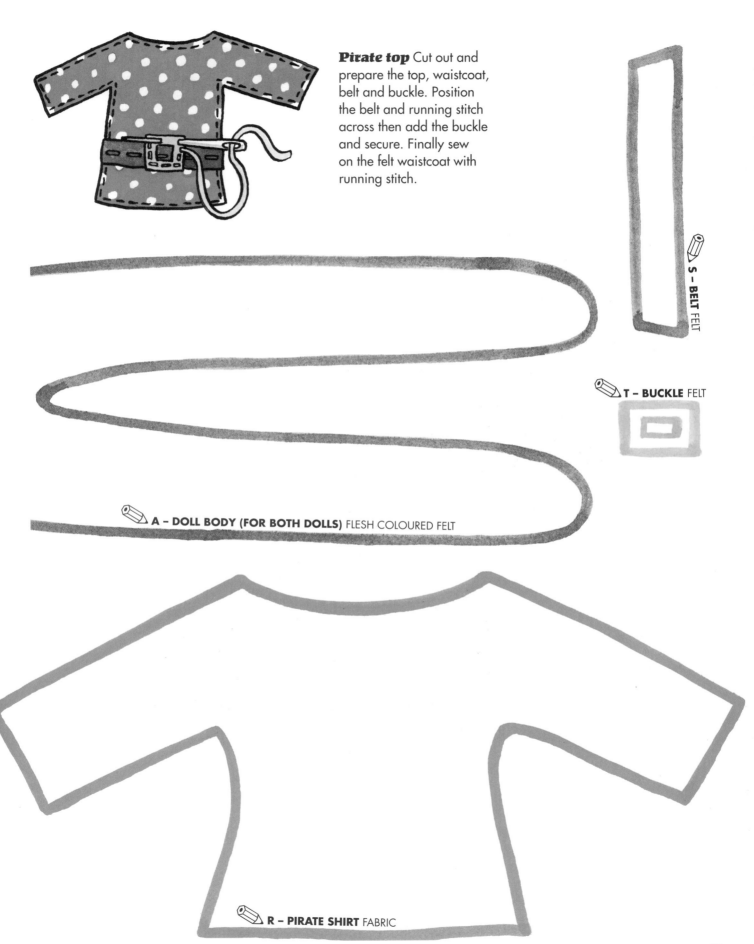

Pirate top Cut out and prepare the top, waistcoat, belt and buckle. Position the belt and running stitch across then add the buckle and secure. Finally sew on the felt waistcoat with running stitch.

S – **BELT** FELT

T – **BUCKLE** FELT

A – **DOLL BODY (FOR BOTH DOLLS)** FLESH COLOURED FELT

R – **PIRATE SHIRT** FABRIC

CLiP CLoP PoNy

CLIP CLOP IS A DELIGHTFUL LITTLE PONY PUPPET WITH A BRILLIANT RED MANE AND SWISHY TAIL. HE IS FAIRLY EASY TO MAKE, SEWN WITH BACKSTITCH EITHER BY HAND OR ON A SEWING MACHINE. GREAT AS A PUPPET, HE WOULD ALSO MAKE A LOVELY CUDDLY TOY.

✎ **What you will need** • SPOTTY PRINT COTTON FABRIC 50 × 90CM (20 × 36IN) • SCRAPS OF FELT IN BLACK AND WHITE • ONE BALL OF CHUNKY WOOL • PLASTIC CURTAIN RINGS 6 × 1CM (2½ × ⅜IN) • WOODEN DOWELS 2 × 30CM (¾ × 12IN) • WAXED COTTON CORD 4.5M (14¾FT) • TOY STUFFING • MULTIPURPOSE POLYESTER THREAD (FOR MACHINE SEWING) OR TOPSTITCHING THREAD (FOR HAND STITCHING) • PLASTIC PAINT BRUSH • HOT GLUE GUN (OPTIONAL) • VANISHING FABRIC PEN

1 Pin and cut out templates A, B and C. Mark the 1cm (³⁄₈in) stitching line on the wrong (back) side with a vanishing fabric pen. On one side of the head shape and the underside of the body mark gaps (for stuffing), using your pattern as a reference.

2 Place right (front) sides together and stitch around the head and body shapes with backstitch (or straight stitch on sewing machine), leaving the gaps open as marked. Sew the legs right sides together, leaving the shorter top edges open. Clip the corners of the head and legs to create sharp points and notch around the head, body and knees. Turn the pieces through to the right side, pushing into the corners with the rounded end of a plastic paintbrush.

3 Stuff the head and body firmly then close the openings with a small overstitch. Lightly stuff the legs halfway, sew across at the halfway mark to create a knee hinge and stuff the remainder. At the top of the legs, turn the edge under by 5mm (¼in) and sew all the way around with a small hand sewn running stitch (gathering). Pull the thread tight, gathering to create the leg shape.

D – OUTER EYE × 2 WHITE FELT

E – INNER EYE × 2 BLACK FELT

F – NOSTRILS × 2 BLACK FELT

"The 1cm (³⁄₈in) stitching line is marked in red. After you have used the template, cut it to this line, place the revised template over your fabric and draw on the line."

STITCHING LINE

TRACE OR PHOTOCOPY THE TEMPLATES AND CUT OUT

C – LEGS × 8 SPOTTY FABRIC

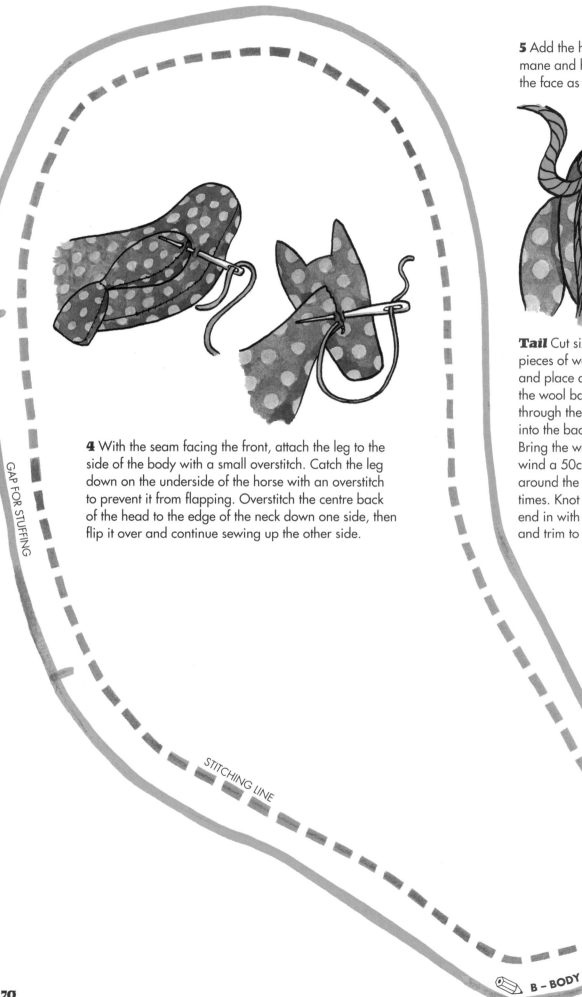

5 Add the hair for the tail, mane and head and decorate the face as follows:

Tail Cut six 36cm (14¼in) pieces of wool then fold in half and place at the back. Flip the wool back and backstitch through the middle point and into the back of the horse. Bring the wool back over and wind a 50cm (20in) length around the top of the tail a few times. Knot the wool, blend the end in with the rest of the tail and trim to neaten.

4 With the seam facing the front, attach the leg to the side of the body with a small overstitch. Catch the leg down on the underside of the horse with an overstitch to prevent it from flapping. Overstitch the centre back of the head to the edge of the neck down one side, then flip it over and continue sewing up the other side.

GAP FOR STUFFING

STITCHING LINE

✏ **B – BODY × 2** SPOTTY FABRIC

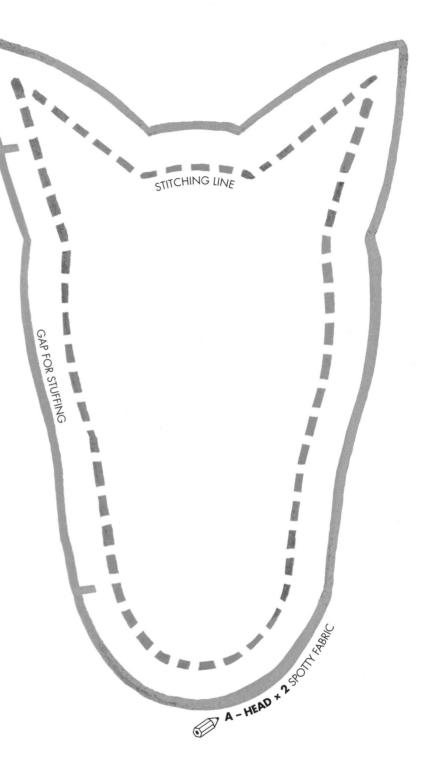

STITCHING LINE

GAP FOR STUFFING

A – HEAD × 2 SPOTTY FABRIC

Mane Cut twenty 16cm (6¼in) pieces of wool, lay out along the centre of the neck and backstitch in place though the wool and body.

Head Cut ten 20cm (8in) pieces of wool. Place so that the first 4cm (1½in) of wool lies over the front of the head and backstitch through the wool and into the head seam. Leave the remaining wool to fall either side of the neck and trim evenly.

Face With a vanishing fabric pen, copy templates D, E and F onto felt, as marked. Running stitch the black inner eye to the white outer eye and overstitch onto the head (just under the fringe of the mane). Overstitch the nostrils onto the bottom of the face.

6 Measure the centre point, 15cm (6in), of each dowel and mark with a pencil. Place a dab of glue in the middle of one (a hot glue gun is ideal) and arrange the dowels in a cross. Wind some waxed cotton cord over the cross point of both dowels and tie with a knot. With an overstitch, sew a plastic ring onto each leg, just above the knee joint, onto the tail and at the back of the head.

7 Cut four 80cm (32in) lengths of waxed cotton cord for each leg. With an adult's help, dab some glue onto the corner points of the dowel. Wind the cord around it a few times and knot, ensuring that the cords are even then tie to each ring on the legs with a knot. Cut two further pieces of cord, 55cm (22in) for the head and 60cm (24in) for the tail. Dab glue on the centre crossing point of the dowel, wind them both around a few times and knot. As before, tie one cord to the back of the head and one to the tail, securing with a knot.

Patchwork BLanket

YOU WILL LEARN:
✔ **PATCHWORK**
✔ **QUILTING**

THIS COLOURFUL BLANKET, MADE FROM SEWING THIRTY SQUARES OF FABRIC TOGETHER, IS A GREAT INTRODUCTION TO PATCHWORKING. A VARIETY OF COLOURED FABRICS CAN LOOK REALLY EYE-CATCHING; WE LINKED OUR FABRICS WITH THREE MAIN COLOURS – PINK, ORANGE AND AQUA.

✎ **What you will need** • TEN COTTON FABRICS IN COMPLEMENTARY PATTERNS AND COLOURS 20 × 60CM (8 × 24IN) • COTTON BACKING FABRIC 77 × 92CM (30¾ × 26¾IN) • COTTON WADDING (BATTING) 77 × 92CM (30¾ × 26¾IN) • 2.8CM (1¹⁄₁₆IN) WIDE BIAS BINDING, TWO 80CM (32IN) LENGTHS AND TWO 95CM (38IN) LENGTHS • TOPSTITCHING THREAD (FOR HAND STITCHING) OR MULTIPURPOSE POLYESTER THREAD (FOR MACHINE STITCHING) • VANISHING FABRIC PEN

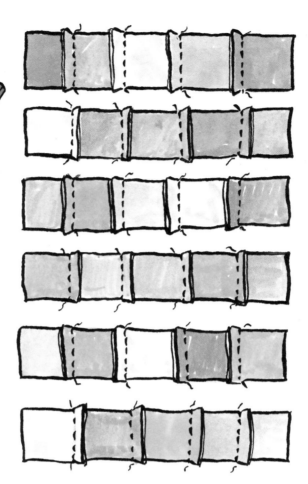

1. Pin template A onto fabric and cut out. Repeat to make three squares of each of your ten different fabrics. Copy template B onto card and lay centrally on the wrong (back) side of each fabric square. Draw around the edge to mark out the 1cm (⅜in) stitching line.

2 Pin the first two squares right (front) sides together along one edge. Sew together along the stitching line, using backstitch by hand or straight stitch by sewing machine. Repeat with the next four squares to create a row of five stitched squares. Repeat with the remaining squares to make six strips of five stitched squares.

3 With an adult's help, take the first strip and press (iron) all the seams to the right. With the next strip, press all the seams to the left. Repeat with the remaining strips to ensure that the seams lie flat. Sew the six strips together in the same way, matching up all the squares. Trim off all threads and press the seams in the same direction.

"The blanket can be sewn entirely by hand or would make an ideal first sewing machine project."

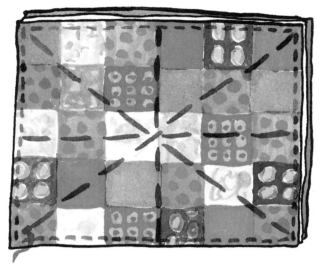

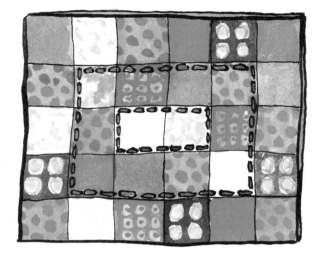

4 Place the backing fabric on a flat surface wrong side up. Place the cotton wadding on top then place the patchwork fabric right side up and pin the three layers together. Using a thread that stands out, sew long running stitches (tacking) across your quilt sandwich, vertically, horizontally and diagonally (these are removed later). In a matching thread, sew a small running stitch about 1cm (⅜in) long and 1cm (⅜in) apart around the outside edge (this will remain in the blanket). Remove all pins.

5 Using a matching coloured topstitching thread, sew quilting stitches (stitches that make a decorative pattern, sewn through all three layers of the quilt sandwich), starting one square in on a corner. Work your way around the blanket with a small running stitch, just inside the seam and repeat on the inner two squares. Remove all tacking stitches.

"When quilting, keep the blanket flat and push your needle in and out to collect four or five stitches at once. Use a thimble to protect your fingers."

6 Cut four lengths of bias binding. Working from the back, pin on the first length and sew in place 1cm (⅜in) from the edge. Fold the binding to the front, turn under 1cm (⅜in) and pin. Trim off any excess. Line up the next strip as before, folding in the end by 1.5cm (⅝in) at the start. Pin and stitch as before and repeat all the way around the edge. Fold in the final end by 1.5cm (⅝in).

7 Working from the front, sew the binding in place with a small running stitch in topstitching thread. Oversew the corners and ask an adult to press.

B – STITCHING GUIDE

A – PATCHWORK SQUARE × 30 FABRIC

TRACE OR PHOTOCOPY THE
TEMPLATES AND CUT OUT

"When choosing your fabrics, choose ones of a similar weight as they are easier to sew together."

Stitch Library

Backstitch

Bring the needle up to the front of the design. Take a backward stitch and then bring the needle up a little way ahead of the first stitch. Insert the needle into the point where the first stitch began and repeat.

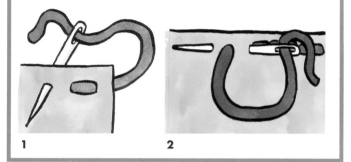

Blanket stitch

Start at the top edge and insert the needle into the front of the fabric. With the point upwards bring the thread, which lies along the top edge, behind the needle and pull through. Repeat.

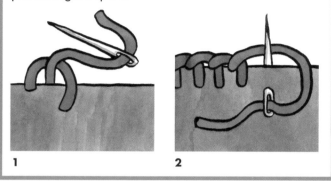

Chain stitch

Bring the thread out and hold down with your thumb. Insert the needle close to where it emerged and bring the point out a little way in front. Pull through, keeping the thread under the needlepoint to form a looped stitch. Repeat.

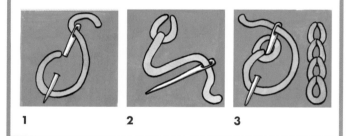

Detached chain stitch and lazy daisy stitch

For detached chain stitch work in the same way as chain stitch but fasten over each loop with a small stitch. Work around in a group to create flower petals known as lazy daisy stitch.

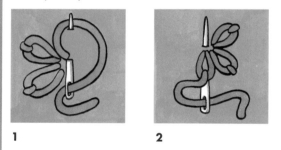

French knots

Bring the needle to the front and hold the thread down with your finger and thumb. Twist the thread around the needle two or three times. Insert the needle close to where the thread emerged and pull the thread tightly through, creating a neat knot on the surface.

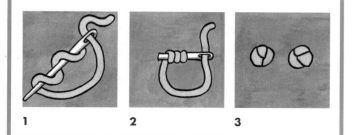

Long (straight) stitch

Worked like a single running stitch. You can create long or short stitches.

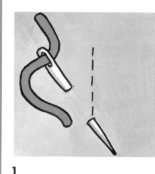
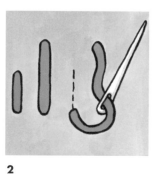

Overstitch

Oversewing stitches join two layers of material. Bring the needle through both pieces of material, close to the edge. Pull the thread through and take back over the top. Repeat.

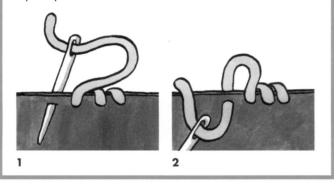

1

2

Running stitch

Take the needle in and out of the fabric, keeping the needle level and pulling the thread through. Keep your stitches small and evenly spaced.

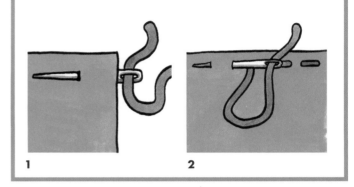

1

2

Satin stitch

Following the outline, bring the needle to the front on one side and take the stitch over to the other side. Continue, keeping the stitches close together and the edges even.

Stem (outline) stitch

Bring the needle up to the front and make a stitch. Bring the needle back up halfway along the first stitch to the left side and make another stitch. Continue with small, even stitches.

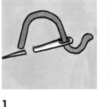 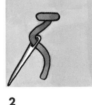 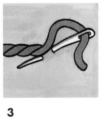

1

2

3

Tacking stitch

Tacking (basting) is done with long, widely spaced stitches, to fasten layers of material together before sewing properly. Take the needle in and out of the fabric and pull the thread through. Stitches should be approximately 1.5cm (⅝in) long and evenly spaced.

 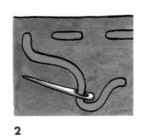

1

2

"If you are right-handed, you will find it easier to sew from right to left and vice versa if you are left-handed."

SUPPLIERS

Doughty's Online

5 Capuchin Yard, Church
Street, Hereford HR1 2LR
Tel: 01432 267542
www.doughtysonline.co.uk

The Eternal Maker

89 Oving Road, Chichester,
West Sussex PO19 7EW
Tel: 01243 788174
www.eternalmaker.com

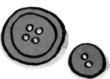

John lewis

Draycott Avenue, London
SW3 2NA
Tel: 08456 049049
www.johnlewis.com

StitchCraftCreate

Brunel House, Newton
Abbot, Devon TQ12 4PU
Tel: 0844 880 5852
www.stitchcraftcreate.co.uk

acknowledgments

Thank you to all of the
inspirational children who
attend our sewing classes
and have been great
helpers, testing many of
the projects in this book.

Thanks also to all at F&W
Media, particularly Sarah,
Pru, James, Ali and our
Editor, Beth, for your
enthusiasm and brilliant
interpretation of our ideas.

Alice: Thank you to all my
boys – you rock!

Ginny: Thank you to my
girls. A special thanks to
Imogen for the use of your
monster design. Thanks
to Mum and Dad for
encouraging my creativity
and to Rod for all your
love and support x

ABOUT THE AUTHORS

Alice Butcher trained as a textile
designer and for many years worked
at Liberty, a famous London store,
running their wonderful Sewing
School. After having her own
children she set up a company with
Ginny making beautiful products
from recycled fabrics. She now
teaches sewing and textile classes to all ages in South East
England. She lives in Surrey with her husband Nick and
sons, Oscar, Edwin and Rufus.

Inspired by her creative mother,
Ginny Farquhar has been sewing
for as long as she can remember.
Early creations were clothes
fashioned for her Pippa dolls and
then later at school she learned to
make clothes for herself. She studied
Costume at Wimbledon School of Art
and enjoyed a successful career creating costumes for the
theatre before setting up a handmade textile business with
Alice in 2001. She lives in Hampshire with two daughters,
two cats and one husband and now spends much of her
time writing craft projects and teaching people how to sew.

Alice and Ginny are lifelong friends, first meeting at
secondary school. They both followed respective careers
in Textiles & Costume before starting their own business
in 2001, creating handmade items from recycled textiles.
They now work together as "Alice and Ginny" sharing
their considerable sewing experience, knowledge and
enthusiasm in sewing classes to learners of all ages. They
have written two further craft books, *Sew Fabulous Fabrics*
and *Home Sweet Sewn*, which have sold over 50,000
copies worldwide.

You can find them at:
www.aliceandginny.co.uk
www.facebook.com/AliceAndGinny
www.twitter.com/aliceandginny

index

A DAVID & CHARLES BOOK
© F&W Media International, Ltd 2013

David & Charles is an imprint of F&W Media International, Ltd
Brunel House, Forde Close, Newton Abbot, TQ12 4PU, UK

F&W Media International, Ltd is a subsidiary of F+W Media, Inc
10151 Carver Road, Suite #200, Blue Ash, OH 45242, USA

Text and Designs © Alice Butcher and Ginny Farquhar 2013
Layout and Photography © F&W Media International, Ltd 2013

First published in the UK and USA in 2013

Alice Butcher and Ginny Farquhar have asserted their right to be identified as authors of this work in
accordance with the Copyright, Designs and Patents Act, 1988.

The author and publisher have made every effort to ensure that all the instructions in the book are accurate
and safe, and therefore cannot accept liability for any resulting injury, damage or loss to persons or property,
however it may arise.

Names of manufacturers and product ranges are provided for the information of readers, with no intention to
infringe copyright or trademarks.

A catalogue record for this book is available from the British Library.

ISBN-13: 978-1-4463-0260-6 hardback
ISBN-10: 1-4463-0260-1 hardback

ISBN-13: 978-1-4463-0261-3 paperback
ISBN-10: 1-4463-0261-X paperback

Printed in China by RR Donnelley for:
F&W Media International, Ltd
Brunel House, Forde Close, Newton Abbot, TQ12 4PU, UK

10 9 8 7 6 5 4 3 2 1

Acquisitions Editor: Sarah Callard
Junior Acquisitions Editor: James Brooks
Project Editor: Beth Dymond
Design Consultant: Prudence Rogers
Photographers: Lorna Yabsley and Jack Gorman
Senior Production Controller: Kelly Smith

F+W Media publishes high quality books on a wide range of subjects.
For more great book ideas visit: www.stitchcraftcreate.co.uk